Slimmer

Eats

COOKBOOK

90+

Weight Loss Recipes: Simple, Healthy, and Delicious

TABLE OF CONTENTS

Breakfast 06

Soup 31

Poultry 49

Beef, lamb & pork 65

Rice, pasta & noodles 89

Sea food 108

Salad 121

Dessert 131

Dear Reader

Welcome to the world of healthy eating and delicious flavors! In this collection of recipes, we invite you on a journey towards a healthier and slimmer you.We've curated a selection of mouthwatering dishes that will tantalize your taste buds while supporting your weight loss goals.

With a focus on wholesome ingredients and smart cooking techniques, these recipes are designed to nourish your body and ignite your culinary creativity. From vibrant salads to hearty soups, from satisfying mains to guilt-free desserts, each dish is thoughtfully crafted to deliver on taste without compromising on nutrition.

Whether you're embarking on a new wellness journey or simply seeking inspiration for wholesome meals, this collection is here to empower and support you. So let's dive into the world of healthy recipes together, and unlock a world of flavor and well-being on your plate. Get ready to savor the joy of nourishing your body and delighting your taste buds with every recipe in this cookbook. Let's embark on this transformative culinary adventure, one delicious dish at a time!

Breakfast

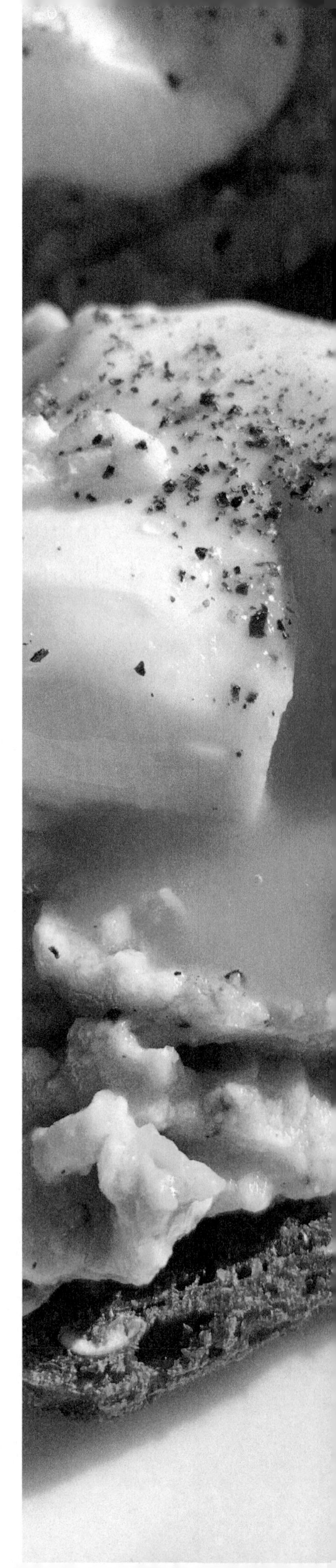

Cooked breakfast

 1 servings 

INGREDIENTS

- 2 Slimming World Pork Sausages
- 2 rashers lean back bacon, visible fat removed
- Low-calorie cooking spray
- Button mushrooms, halved
- 1 small onion, cut into rings
- 1 tomato, halved
- 1 medium boiled potato, cubed
- ½ can baked beans
- 1 or 2 large eggs*

DIRECTIONS

1. Preheat your grill to medium-hot. Cook the sausages according to the pack instructions, turning frequently, adding the bacon for the final 10 minutes of cooking time and turning the bacon halfway.
2. Meanwhile, spray a non-stick frying pan with low-calorie cooking spray and place over a medium-high heat. Add the mushrooms, onion, tomato and potato and fry until everything has softened and the potato is golden brown.
3. Heat the beans in a small pan until piping hot.
4. Crack the eggs into a non-stick pan and cook to your liking. Assemble your breakfast on a large plate, adding brown sauce or tomato ketchup if you fancy it (1 Syn per level tbsp).

Avocado breakfast bowl

 2 serving  45 minutes

INGREDIENTS

- 2 back bacon rashers, visible fat removed
- Low-calorie cooking spray
- 200g of your favourite mushrooms, halved or chopped
- 100g baby spinach
- 8 cherry tomatoes
- 100g lean ham, visible fat removed, diced or chopped
- 2 eggs*
- ½ avocado, sliced
- 1 tbsp chopped fresh chives

*Pregnant women, the elderly, babies and toddlers are advised to choose eggs showing the British Lion stamp if eating raw or partially cooked eggs.

DIRECTIONS

1. Preheat your grill to high and your oven to 220°C/fan 200°C/gas 7.
2. Grill the bacon for 2-3 minutes on each side then roughly chop and set aside.
3. Meanwhile, spray a non-stick frying pan with low-calorie cooking spray and place over a medium-high heat. Add the mushrooms and stir-fry for 5 minutes or until softened and browned. Transfer to a plate and set aside.
4. Wipe the pan. Rinse the spinach under cold water, drain in a sieve and add to the frying pan. Cook for 1-2 minutes or until just wilted, stirring all the time, then transfer to the plate with the mushrooms.
5. Wipe the pan, reduce the heat to medium and stir-fry the tomatoes gently for about 5 minutes, so that they take on some colour but keep their shape.
6. Mix the bacon, mushrooms, spinach, tomatoes and ham and season lightly. Divide the mixture between 2 x 500ml gratin dishes, each about 16cm across and 5cm deep (or see tip). Cover each dish with foil and bake for 10 minutes or until piping hot.
7. Remove the foil, crack an egg into the centre of each dish and return to the oven to cook, uncovered, for 12-15 minutes or until the eggs are cooked to your liking. Divide the avocado slices evenly and scatter over the chives to serve.

Tiramisu Weetabix cheesecake

 1 serving  10 minutes+ 12 hours chilling

INGREDIENTS

- 2 Weetabix
- 2 tbsp fat-free natural yogurt
- 1 tsp instant coffee granules, dissolved in 1 tsp boiling water
- 160g no-added-sugar fat-free vanilla yogurt
- ½ level tsp cocoa powderc)

DIRECTIONS

1. Put the Weetabix in a bowl and crush them with your hands or a fork. Add the natural yogurt and mix together.
2. Spoon the mixture into the base of a dessert glass and press down firmly.
3. Stir the coffee into the vanilla yogurt and pour it over the base to form a second layer. Cover and chill overnight.
4. Sprinkle over the cocoa powder and serve.

Banoffee Weetabix cheesecake

 1 serving 10 minutes+ 12 hours chilling

INGREDIENTS

- 2 Weetabix
- 2 tbsp fat-free natural yogurt
- 160g no-added-sugar fat-free toffee yogurt
- 1 banana, sliced
- 1 level tsp ChocShot

DIRECTIONS

1. Put the Weetabix in a bowl and crush them with your hands or a fork. Add the natural yogurt and mix together.
2. Spoon the mixture into the base of a dessert glass and press down firmly.
3. Pour the toffee yogurt over the base to form a second layer. Cover and chill overnight.
4. Top with the sliced banana and ChocShot to serve.

Overnight oats

 1 serving  10 minutes+ 12 hours chilling

INGREDIENTS

- 40g plain porridge oats
- 2-3 fresh nectarines, stoned and sliced
- ½ tsp vanilla extract
- 200g fat-free natural Greek yogurt (or dairy-free soya yogurt, plain and unsweetened, with added calcium, if you need this to be vegan)
- Pinch of ground cinnamon

DIRECTIONS

1. Put half of the oats in a lidded jar or bowl and top with half of the sliced nectarines.
2. Stir the vanilla extract and 3 tbsp water into the yogurt and spoon half into the jar or bowl.
3. Add the rest of the oats, most of the remaining fruit and the rest of the yogurt. Top with the rest of the fruit, sprinkle with ground cinnamon and chill overnight. Stir it all together when you're ready to eat.

Baked oats

 1 serving  40 minutes

INGREDIENTS

- 40g plain porridge oats
- 1 level tsp sweetener
- 1 small egg
- 100g fat-free natural yogurt
- Few drops of vanilla essence
- 100g raspberries

DIRECTIONS

1. Preheat your oven to 200°C/fan 180°C/gas 6.
2. Place all the ingredients in a bowl and mix together well. Transfer the mixture to a small ovenproof dish (we used an individual casserole dish) and bake in the oven for 35 minutes, or until browned.
3. Serve with lots of Speed Free Food fruits.

Microwave scrambled eggs

 1 serving  4 minutes

INGREDIENTS

- 2 eggs
- 2 tbsp whole milk
- toast, to serve

DIRECTIONS

1. Use a fork to beat together the eggs, milk and a pinch of salt in a microwave-safe jug. Cook in the microwave on High for 30 seconds, then beat again and return to the microwave for another 30 seconds.
2. Beat again, breaking up any lumps of egg. Microwave for another 15 seconds, then beat again; the eggs will be loose at this stage so serve them straightaway if this is how you like them. If you prefer your eggs a little firmer, microwave for a further 15 seconds, beat, then serve.

Baked eggs with spinach, tomatoes, ricotta & basil

 4 serving  40 minutes

INGREDIENTS

- 2 tbsp olive oil
- 1 onion, finely chopped
- 1 garlic clove, crushed
- pinch of chilli flakes
- 3 x 400g cans finely chopped tomatoes (or blitz regular canned chopped tomatoes using a food processor or hand blender)
- 3 tbsp sundried tomato pesto (ensure vegetarian, if needed)
- 200g spinach, roughly chopped
- 8 eggs
- 100g ricotta
- 40g parmesan or vegetarian alternative, finely grated
- handful of basil leaves
- crusty bread or focaccia, to serve

DIRECTIONS

1. Heat the oil in a large, shallow, flameproof casserole or frying pan over a low-medium heat and fry the onion with a pinch of salt for 10 mins until soft and translucent. Add the garlic and chilli flakes, and fry for 1 min more. Tip in the tomatoes, 1 tsp sugar and pesto. Season and simmer, uncovered, for 10 mins, stirring often. Tip in the spinach and cook for another 5 mins until wilted.
2. Heat the grill to high. Make eight gaps in the sauce with the back of a spoon and crack an egg into each. Dot over the ricotta and scatter with the parmesan. Cover and cook for 5 mins, then slide under the hot grill for a few minutes until the egg whites are set and the yolks runny. Scatter with the basil and serve with crusty bread for dunking.

Breakfast Muffins

 4 serving  40 minutes

INGREDIENTS

- Low-calorie cooking spray
- 250g mushrooms, diced or sliced
- 120g lean ham, visible fat removed, roughly chopped
- 4 spring onions, finely chopped
- 8 eggs
- 3 level tbsp skimmed milk

DIRECTIONS

1. Preheat your oven to 200°C/fan 180°C/gas 6.
2. Spray a non-stick frying pan with low-calorie cooking spray and place over a medium heat. Fry the mushrooms for 10 minutes or until golden. Stir in the ham and spring onions.
3. Put the eggs and milk in a bowl, season lightly and whisk well.
4. Spray 8 holes of a reliably non-stick muffin tin with low-calorie cooking spray. Spoon in the mushroom mixture and pour in the eggs. Bake for 20-25 minutes or until golden and slightly risen.
5. Leave to cool slightly before easing the muffins out of the tin. Serve them warm or leave to cool completely, then store in an airtight container in the fridge for up to 3 days and enjoy either cold or thoroughly reheated.

Blueberry smoothie

1 serving 5 minutes

INGREDIENTS

- 175g blueberries
- 1 small banana, sliced
- 1 tbsp natural or Greek yogurt
- 100ml apple juice, chilled
- 3-4 mint leaves (optional), plus extra to garnish

DIRECTIONS

1. Put the blueberries, banana, yogurt, apple juice and mint, if using, in a blender and blitz until smooth. Add a splash of water if it seems too thick.
2. Pour the smoothie into a tall glass with a glass straw to serve. Garnish with a sprig of mint, if you like.

Breakfast Quiche

 6 servings  40 minutes

INGREDIENTS

- 2 low fat sausages cooked and sliced
- 5 bacon medallions cooked
- 6 - 8 mushrooms sliced
- 3 tomatoes sliced
- 8 eggs
- 2 tbsp quark
- sea salt
- freshly ground black pepper
- 1 sprig fresh parsley chopped

DIRECTIONS

1. Pre heat the oven to 190°c.
2. Cook the sausages and bacon medallions. You can do this in advance and keep them in the fridge until you're ready for them.
3. Arrange the sausage slices in the bottom of an 8 inch round silicone cake mould. Place the cooked bacon medallions on top, followed by the sliced mushrooms then the sliced tomatoes.
4. Crack the eggs into a large bowl or jug, add the quark and some salt and pepper, then whisk until they mixed well and there's no lumps or quark. Pour the eggs into the cake mould, then sprinkle the chopped parsley on top.
5. Cook at 190°C for 25 - 30 minutes, or until the quiche is set and golden in colour.
6. Serve warm or cold with a good helping of vegetables!

Banana overnight oats

2 servings 5 minutes

INGREDIENTS

- 2 bananas, peeled
- 100g porridge oats
- ¼ tsp ground cinnamon, plus a pinch to serve
- 1 tbsp maple syrup
- 300ml milk of your choice, plus a splash
- 2 tbsp peanut or almond butter, plus extra to serve
- 2 tbsp flaked or chopped almonds
- 2-4 tbsp natural yogurt, to serve (optional)

DIRECTIONS

1. Mash 1 banana in a bowl with a fork until smooth. Stir in the oats, cinnamon, maple syrup, milk and peanut butter. Mix well, then cover and chill overnight.
2. The next morning, stir the porridge, adding another splash of milk if the mixture is quite stiff. Divide between two bowls. Slice the remaining banana and scatter this over the porridge, drizzle with more nut butter and sprinkle over the almonds. Top with spoonfuls of yogurt, if using, and sprinkle with a pinch more cinnamon before serving.

Simit poğaçaa

 22 servings  3 hours

INGREDIENTS

- 350ml whole milk
- 7g sachet fast-action dried yeast
- 2 tsp caster sugar
- 2 egg yolks (freeze the whites for another recipe)
- 500g strong white bread flour, plus extra for dusting
- 115g unsalted butter, at room temperature, cut into pieces
- 1 egg, beaten
- 1 tsp sesame seeds
- 1 tsp nigella seeds
- 125g marinated black olives, pitted and chopped (see tip, below)
- 125g feta, crumbled
- 125g cheddar, grated
- ½ small bunch of parsley, chopped
- 75g Turkish pepper paste

DIRECTIONS

1. Heat the milk in a heatproof bowl in the microwave or in a pan over a low heat until lukewarm. Add the yeast and sugar, then leave to stand for 15 mins until frothy. Tip the egg yolks, flour, butter and ½ tsp salt into the bowl of a stand mixer fitted with a dough hook, and add the warm milk mixture. Knead for 10 mins – the dough should be tacky. Or, knead by hand for about 15 mins.
2. Cover and leave to prove for at least 1-2 hrs until doubled in size, or chill overnight. If you're proving at room temperature, chill the dough for 30 mins after it has doubled to make it easier to work with.
3. Meanwhile, prepare the filling. Combine the olives, both the cheeses and the parsley, then set aside. Roll the dough out on a lightly floured work surface into a large rectangle (about 46 x 30cm).
4. Spread the pepper paste all over the dough. With a long side facing you, scatter half the filling over the half of the rectangle that's closest to you, then fold the other half over that to enclose the filling. Gently roll out the dough again to help the filling stick to the dough, then cut the rectangle vertically into 20 x 2½cm strips. Working with one strip at a time, fold the strip loosely in half, then holding it at both ends, twist, then gently pull the loose ends through the loop.
5. Heat the oven to 220C/200C fan/gas 8 and line a baking sheet with baking parchment. Lay the simit on the sheet and brush with the beaten egg. Sprinkle over the sesame and nigella seeds, then leave to rest on the baking sheet for about 20 mins.
6. Bake for 25-30 mins, or until golden brown. Leave to cool slightly on the sheet before serving.

Protein pancakes

 2 servings  15 minutes

INGREDIENTS

- 1 banana
- 75g oats
- 3 large eggs
- 2 tbsp milk (dairy, soya, oat or nut milks all work)
- 1 tbsp baking powder
- pinch of cinnamon
- 2 tbsp protein powder (whey, pea or whatever your preference)
- coconut oil, or a flavourless oil, for frying
- nut butter, maple syrup and berries or sliced banana to serve

DIRECTIONS

1. Whizz the banana, oats, eggs, milk, baking powder, cinnamon and protein powder in a blender for 1-2 mins until smooth. Check the oats have broken down, if not, blend for another minute.
2. Heat a drizzle of oil in a pan. Pour or ladle in 2-3 rounds of batter, leaving a little space between each to spread. Cook for 1-2 minutes, until bubbles start to appear on the surface and the underside is golden. Flip over and cook for another minute until cooked through. Transfer to a warmed oven and repeat with the remaining batter. Serve in stacks with nut butter, maple syrup and fruit.

Soufflé pancakes

 1 serving  30 minutes

INGREDIENTS

- 2 large eggs, separated
- 2 tbsp golden caster sugar
- 1 tsp vanilla extract
- 2 tbsp milk
- 2 tbsp self-raising flour
- 1 tsp vegetable oil
- butter, icing sugar and maple syrup, to serve

DIRECTIONS

1. Whisk the egg whites in a clean bowl with 1 tbsp sugar using an electric whisk or a stand mixer to form stiff peaks.
2. Beat the egg yolks, 1 tbsp sugar and vanilla together in a separate bowl until pale and foamy, and a ribbon trail is left on the surface when the beaters are removed. Gently fold in the milk and flour until just incorporated.
3. Fold the egg whites into the egg yolk mixture and gently turn the batter over to mix, using the side of a metal spoon or spatula to keep all the air in the mixture.
4. Working fairly quickly, heat a large non-stick pan with a lid over a very low heat. Drizzle a little oil into the pan, then wipe it with a piece of kitchen paper – you only want a small film on the base of the pan. Make three tall pancakes by piling three spoonfuls of the batter into the pan, using about two thirds of the mixture. Keep them piled quite high, don't tip the pan or spread them out like you would normal pancakes. Cover with a lid and cook for 2-4 mins, the steam will help them set. Remove the lid and add another dollop of batter to each pancake, this will create the classic height and thickness. Return the lid and cook for another 4-6 mins until the top feels slightly set.
5. Very gently, and carefully, turn the pancakes over in the pan with a fish slice or spatula. The bases should be a light golden brown. Add the lid back on and cook for another 4-6 mins until both sides are golden brown and they have a slight wobble, but are not collapsing or sticky. Serve with a pat of butter, a dusting of icing sugar and a little maple syrup.

Mincemeat banana bread

 8 servings  1 hour 20 minutes

INGREDIENTS

- 150g unsalted butter, softened, plus extra for the tin
- 90g caster sugar
- 2 large eggs, beaten
- 150g self-raising flour
- 1 tsp baking powder
- 1 tsp mixed spice
- 2 ripe bananas (200g), peeled and mashed
- 150g mincemeat (ensure it's vegetarian, if needed)
- 100g salted butter, softened
- 2 tbsp honey
- 2 tsp ground cinnamon

DIRECTIONS

1. Heat the oven to 180C/160C fan/gas 4. Butter a 900g loaf tin and line the base and sides with baking parchment. Set aside.
2. Beat the butter and sugar with an electric whisk until light and fluffy, then slowly whisk in the beaten egg, followed by half the flour. Fold in the remaining flour, the baking powder, mixed spice, mashed bananas and mincemeat.
3. Pour into the tin and bake for 1 hr until a skewer inserted into the middle comes out clean (cover with foil if it darkens too quickly). Leave to cool in the tin for 10 mins, then transfer to a wire rack and leave to cool completely.
4. To make the whipped butter, beat the butter, honey and cinnamon using an electric whisk until pale and fluffy. If you like, toast slices of the bread and spread with the butter while warm. The bread will keep in an airtight container for three days, and the butter chilled for up to five.

Kimchi scrambled eggs

 1 serving 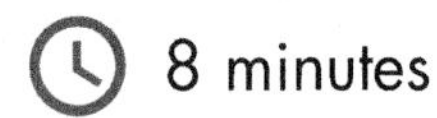

INGREDIENTS

- 2 medium eggs
- 1 tbsp milk
- 40g kimchi
- 1 slice of wholemeal bread, toasted
- 1 spring onion, finely sliced
- pinch of togarashi, to serve (optional)

DIRECTIONS

1. Beat the eggs and milk together with a pinch of salt. Pour into a non-stick pan over a low heat. Leave untouched for 30 seconds, then lift the pan a little and swirl the eggs around. Cook for 2 mins more, then fold through the kimchi, breaking up the eggs to scramble them.
2. Serve the kimchi scrambled eggs on the toast, and top with the spring onion and tograshi, if using.

Blueberry & banana smoothie

 2 serving  5 minutes

INGREDIENTS

- 2 ripe bananas, peeled
- 125g blueberries (fresh or frozen)
- 300g pack silken tofu, drained
- 2 tbsp porridge oats

DIRECTIONS

1. Whizz all of the ingredients together in a blender with 300ml water. Drink straight away or transfer to a bottle for later, shaking well before drinking.

Raspberry, almond & oat breakfast cookies

 12 cookies  25 minutes

INGREDIENTS

- 2 ripe bananas, mashed
- 150g porridge oats
- 2 tbsp ground almonds
- ½ tsp cinnamon
- 100g raspberries (fresh or frozen)

DIRECTIONS

1. Heat the oven to 200C/180C fan/gas 4 and line two baking trays with baking parchment. Mix the banana, oats, almonds, cinnamon and a pinch of salt in a bowl to make a sticky dough. Gently stir through the raspberries, trying not to break them up. Scoop up tablespoons of the mixture and roll into balls, then place on a baking tray and flatten with your hand.
2. Bake for 15 mins until the cookies feel firm around the edges and are golden brown. Leave to cool. Will keep in an airtight container for up to three days.

Healthy porridge bowl

 2 servings  15 minutes

INGREDIENTS

- 100g frozen raspberries
- 1 orange, ½ sliced and ½ juiced
- 150g porridge oats
- 100ml milk
- ½ banana, sliced
- 2 tbsp smooth almond butter
- 1 tbsp goji berries
- 1 tbsp chia seeds

DIRECTIONS

1. Tip half the raspberries and all of the orange juice in a pan. Simmer until the raspberries soften, about 5 mins.
2. Meanwhile stir the oats, milk and 450ml water in a pan over a low heat until creamy. Top with the raspberry compote, remaining raspberries, orange slices, banana, almond butter, goji berries and chia seeds.

Three-grain porridge

 18 servings  10 minutes

INGREDIENTS

- 300g oatmeal
- 300g spelt flakes
- 300g barley flakes
- agave nectar and sliced strawberries, to serve (optional)

DIRECTIONS

1. Working in batches, toast the oatmeal, spelt flakes and barley in a large, dry frying pan for 5 mins until golden, then leave to cool and store in an airtight container.
2. When you want to eat it, simply combine 50g of the porridge mixture in a saucepan with 300ml milk or water. Cook for 5 mins, stirring occasionally, then top with a drizzle of honey and strawberries, if you like (optional). Will keep for 6 months.

Bircher muesli with apple & banana

2 servings 5 minutes

INGREDIENTS

- 1 eating apple, coarsely grated
- 50g jumbo porridge oats
- 25g mixed seeds (such as sunflower, pumpkin, sesame and linseed)
- 25g mixed nuts (such as Brazils, hazelnuts, almonds, pecans and walnuts), roughly chopped
- ¼ tsp ground cinnamon
- 100g full-fat natural bio-yogurt
- 1 medium banana, sliced
- 25g organic sultanas

DIRECTIONS

1. Put the grated apple in a bowl and add the oats, seeds, half the nuts and the cinnamon. Toss together well. Stir in the yogurt and 100ml cold water, cover and chill for several hours or overnight. Spoon the muesli into two bowls and top with the sliced banana, sultanas and remaining nuts.

Pineapple smoothie

 1 serving  5 minutes

INGREDIENTS

- 150g pineapple, trimmed, peeled and chopped
- 1 small banana, peeled and sliced
- 1 lime, juiced
- ice (optional)

DIRECTIONS

1. Blitz the pineapple in a blender with the banana, lime juice and 50ml cold water until smooth.
2. Fill a tall glass with ice, if you like, pour over the smoothie and serve immediately.

Vanilla & cinnamon breakfast rice

 4 servings  45 minutes

INGREDIENTS

- 200g wholemeal basmati rice
- 200ml whole milk
- 2 tsp vanilla extract
- 3 bay leaves
- 1 cinnamon stick
- 12 dried apricots split in half widthways (so they still look whole)
- 4 x 100ml pots bio yogurt
- 12 walnut halves, broken into pieces

DIRECTIONS

1. Tip the rice into a large, deep non-stick pan with 600ml water, the milk, vanilla, bay leaves and cinnamon stick. Bring to the boil, then cover with a lid and simmer for 25-30 mins until the rice is tender. Keep an eye on it to ensure it doesn't boil dry towards the end of its cooking time.
2. Meanwhile, tip the apricots into a small pan with 300ml water and cook over a low-medium heat until tender, about 10-15 mins. Set aside.
3. Remove the bay leaves and cinnamon stick from the rice, then stir in half the yogurt. Both the rice and the apricots will keep chilled, separately, for up to 24 hrs. Spoon the rice into bowls and top with the remaining yogurt, the apricots and their juices and the walnuts. If you've prepared the rice and apricots the day before, eat cold or reheat until warm, adding a splash of milk to the rice to loosen.

Soups

Cauliflower cheese soup 31
Tomato & basil soup 32
Leek & potato soup 33
Carrot & corriander soup 34
Roasted pumpkin soup 35
Sweetcorn & leek soup 36
Spicy chicken & vegetable soup 37
Chicken vegetable pasta soup 38
Chicken & lentil soup 39
Hearty vegetable soup 40
Split pea & bacon soup 41
Turkey taco soup 42
Chicken chickpeas spinach soup 43
Chicken noodle soup 44
Chicken tortilla soup 45
Sweet potato red pepper & carrot soup 46
Coconut chicken rice soup 47

Cauliflower cheese soup

 4 servings  40 minutes

INGREDIENTS

- Low-calorie cooking spray
- 1 large onion, peeled and finely chopped
- ½ tsp smoked paprika
- 550g small cauliflower florets
- 800ml vegetable stock
- 10 The Laughing Cow Extra Light Cheese Triangles
- Smoked paprika, to serve

DIRECTIONS

1. Spray a large non-stick saucepan with low-calorie cooking spray and heat gently. Add the onion and paprika and cook for 5 minutes, stirring occasionally, until softened slightly.
2. Add the cauliflower and stock and bring to the boil. Cover and simmer for 15 minutes until the cauliflower is just tender. Using a slotted spoon, lift out a few cauliflower florets and set aside to garnish. Stir the cheese triangles into the soup and blend with a stick blender or in a food processor until smooth. Season lightly.
3. To serve, divide between shallow bowls and top with the cauliflower florets. Sprinkle with smoked paprika and serve immediately.

Tomato and basil soup

 4 servings  45 minutes

INGREDIENTS

- 1 large onion, chopped
- 2 carrots, chopped
- 3 celery sticks, chopped
- 2 garlic cloves, crushed
- 1.2 litres hot vegetable stock, suitable for vegans
- 900g ripe tomatoes, chopped
- 400g can chopped tomatoes
- 500g passata
- 1 red pepper, deseeded and chopped
- 1 tbsp tomato purée
- ½ small pack fresh basil leaves

DIRECTIONS

1. Put the onion, carrots, celery and garlic in a large non-stick saucepan. Pour in the stock and bring to the boil over a high heat. Reduce the heat to low and simmer for 20 minutes or until the vegetables are soft.
2. Add the fresh tomatoes, canned tomatoes, passata, red pepper and tomato purée and simmer for 10 minutes.
3. Remove from the heat and add the basil, reserving a few leaves. Blitz until smooth with a stick blender (or use a food processor and return to the pan).
4. Season to taste and divide between bowls. Chop the remaining basil and scatter over the bowls to serve.

Leek and potato soup

INGREDIENTS

- 1 large onion, finely chopped
- 1 garlic clove, finely chopped
- 2 bay leaves
- 1.2 litres hot chicken or vegetable stock
- 700g potatoes, finely diced
- 1 large leek, sliced lengthways, then shredded
- 1 tsp dried mixed herbs
- 150g fat-free natural fromage frais
- 2 tbsp chopped fresh chives

DIRECTIONS

1. Place the onion and garlic in a large saucepan along with the bay leaves and 150ml of the stock. Bring to the boil, cover and simmer for 5 minutes.
2. Add the potato and all but a few shreds of the leek. Pour in the remaining stock, add the dried herbs and season lightly. Bring to the boil, cover and simmer for 25 minutes until tender.
3. Discard the bay leaves and transfer the mixture to a food processor or blender. Blend until smooth and return to the saucepan.
4. Blend in the fromage frais and reheat gently without boiling. Adjust the seasoning if necessary. Ladle into bowls and top with the reserved shredded leek and chopped chives.

Carrot and coriander soup

 4 servings  45 minutes

INGREDIENTS

- 1 large onion, chopped
- 80g peeled butternut squash, chopped
- 750g carrots, peeled and chopped
- 1 litre boiling vegetable stock
- 1 tsp ground coriander
- 60g canned cannellini beans, drained
- 10g fresh coriander, finely chopped
- 3 tbsp plain quark

DIRECTIONS

1. Put the onion into a large pan with the squash, carrots, stock and ground coriander. Bring to the boil over a high heat, turn the heat to low and simmer for 20 minutes or until the vegetables are very soft.
2. Add the beans to the soup and simmer for 2 minutes. Take off the heat, cool slightly, then pour into a food processor or liquidiser and whizz until smooth.
3. Stir in the coriander and quark, season to taste and serve.

Roasted Pumpkin Soup

 4 servings  55 minutes

INGREDIENTS

- 2kg of sugar (pie pumpkins)
- 1-2 tsps of paprika
- salt and black pepper
- 1 leek, sliced
- 2 stalks of celery
- 1 onion, chopped
- 2 cloves of garlic, crushed
- 1 tsp of fresh grated ginger
- 4 cups of vegetable stock
- spray oil

DIRECTIONS

1. Preheat oven to 200c/400g
2. Cut pumpkins in half, remove seeds, then slice pumpkin, season with paprika, salt and pepper, place on a baking tray lined with parchment paper and spray with spray oil
3. Roast in the oven for 30 mins
4. While the pumpkin is roasting, spray a deep saucepan with some spray oil, add the onion, garlic, ginger, celery and leeks and fry to soften
5. Pour in the stock, bring to a boil and simmer until pumpkin is cooked.
6. Allow pumpkin to cool slightly and then peel off skins.
7. Add to a blender along with the soup base, and blend till smooth.
8. Add back to the pan and simmer just until thickened and creamy.
9. Season as need with salt and black pepper.

Sweetcorn and Leek Soup

 4 servings  35 minutes

INGREDIENTS

- 2 medium leeks, sliced
- 1 onion, finely chopped
- 2 cups (480ml) of cooked corn (fresh, frozen or canned)
- 4 spring onions, finely sliced
- 4 cups (960ml) of vegetable stock/broth
- salt and black pepper
- spray oil

DIRECTIONS

1. Spray a deep saucepan with some spray oil
2. Add the onion and leek and fry for approx 5 mins to soften
3. Season with salt and black pepper
4. Stir in the corn and stock
5. Bring to a boil and cover and simmer for approx 15 mins.
6. Add ¾ of the soup to a blender and blend till smooth.
7. Add back to the remaining soup and continue to simmer for about 5 mins just until it thickens.
8. Ladle into bowls and serve topped with the chopped spring onion.

Spicy Chicken and Vegetable Soup

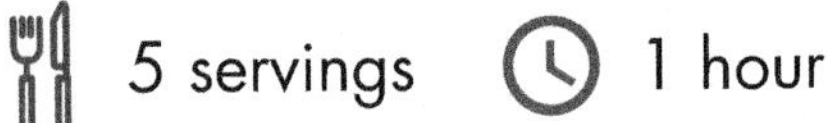
5 servings 1 hour

INGREDIENTS

- 1 onion, diced finely
- 2 cloves of garlic, crushed
- 2 tsp of freshly grated ginger
- 1 leek, sliced
- 1 large carrot, diced
- 200g (7oz) of zucchini (courgette), diced
- 300g (10.5oz) of butternut squash, diced
- 1 red pepper, diced
- 1 cup (240ml) of passata)
- 6 cups (1.44 litres) of chicken stock
- 1 tbs of cumin
- 1 tbs of coriander
- 1 tsp of turmeric
- 1 tsp of paprika
- ¼ tsp of cayenne (reduce or increase depending on how spicy you like it)
- 300g (10.5oz) of cooked shredded chicken (I use a mixture of breast and thigh meat)
- salt and black pepper
- ½ cup (120ml) of fresh coriander (cilantro), chopped (optional)
- spray oil

DIRECTIONS

1. Spray a deep pot over a medium high heat with spray oil
2. Add the onion, leek and carrot, season with salt and pepper and fry for a minute
3. Add a little bit of stock (approx ¼ cup - 60ml), and reduce it down, till onions, leeks are translucent.
4. Add the garlic and ginger and saute for 1 minute
5. Add the butternut squash, red pepper and zucchini.
6. Stir in the spices
7. Add the passata and stock.
8. Bring to a boil, reduce heat, cover and simmer for 30 mins
9. Roughly blend with an immersion stick blender (or add half the soup to a regular blender, blend till smooth and return to the pot)
10. Add the chicken and cilantro (coriander), and mix to combine, stirring till heated through.
11. Ladle into bowls and enjoy!!

Chicken Vegetable Pasta Soup

 6 servings  30 minutes

INGREDIENTS

- 400g/14oz of boneless skinless chicken thigh
- 200g/7oz of uncooked pasta
- 250g/9oz of butternut squash diced
- 200g/7oz of carrots, diced
- 200g/7oz of celery, diced
- 1 onion, diced
- 2 cloves of garlic, crushed
- 1 tsp of paprika
- 1 tsp of mixed herbs
- pinch of chilli powder
- pinch of cumin
- 8.5 cups/2 litres of chicken stock
- ½ cup of frozen peas
- fresh chopped parsley
- cooking oil spray
- salt and black pepper

DIRECTIONS

1. Spray a large pot over a medium high heat with cooking oil spray
2. Add the chicken, paprika, chilli, cumin, onion powder, a little salt and black pepper and cook until browned, remove and set aside.
3. Spray the pot with a little more cooking oil spray, add the onion, celery and carrot and a little of the stock to deglaze the pan and fry for a couple of minutes until the onion is translucent.
4. Add the butternut squash and garlic, return the chicken, add the mixed herbs and stock, bring to boil and simmer for about 8 mins until the vegetables are tender.
5. Add in the uncooked pasta and simmer continue to simmer for about 10-12 minutes until the pasta is al dente
6. Stir in the peas and a little fresh parsley, season as needed with salt and black pepper.

Chicken and Lentil Soup

 4 servings  5 hour 20 minutes

INGREDIENTS

for the soup base:

- 1 Roast Chicken Carcass
- 1 onion, chopped
- 2 carrots, chopped
- 2 cloves of garlic, finely chopped
- 1 tablespoon of mixed herbs (rosemary, thyme, oregano)
- 1 tsp of salt
- pinch of black pepper

for the soup:

- 1 onion, finely chopped
- 2 carrots, finely chopped
- 1 stick of celery finely, chopped
- 2 tsp of ground cumin
- 2 tsp of ground coriander
- 250g (10.5oz) of leftover cooked chicken
- ½ cup (120g) of dry red lentils (rinsed)
- salt and black pepper
- cooking oil spray
- fresh chopped parsley

DIRECTIONS

1. Spray a large pot with cooking oil spray over a medium high heat, add the onion, carrots, garlic and mixed herbs and fry for a few mins to soften. Break up the chicken carcass and add to the pot. Fry for a further few mins.
2. Cover with 2 litres of water and add the salt and black pepper. Bring to a boil and then reduce heat to low, cover and simmer for approx 2-4 hours (the longer you can simmer the better, as it improves the flavour of the base, If you haven't got a chicken carcass, you can use 2 litres of ready made chicken stock)
3. Drain the soup base over a sieve, so that you just have the liquid/stock and set aside.
4. Clean pot and spray with some cooking oil spray, add the onion, carrots and celery and fry for approx 5 mins to soften.
5. Add the cumin and coriander and stir to coat.
6. Pour in the stock and lentils and bring to a boil, simmer for approx 45 mins, until lentils are softened.
7. Add in the chicken and a handful of fresh chopped parsley and continue to simmer for approx 10 mins
8. Season as needed with salt and black pepper.

Hearty Vegetable Soup

 4 servings  1 hour 5 minutes

INGREDIENTS

- 1 onion, chopped finely
- 2 cloves of garlic, crushed
- 1 large leek, sliced finely
- 2 sticks of celery, chopped
- 2 carrots, chopped
- 250g of potato, peeled and chopped into small cubes (use a waxy variety)
- 1 litre of chicken or vegetable stock
- 2 bay leaves
- a couple of sprigs of fresh thyme (or 1 tsp of dried)
- optional: a pinch of chilli flakes
- salt and pepper to season
- fresh chopped parsley
- cooking oil spray (I used avocado spray oil)

DIRECTIONS

1. Spray a large saucepan over medium heat with some cooking oil spray and add the onions, garlic and celery.
2. Fry for a couple of minutes to soften. Add in a little stock at a time and reduce down to prevent any burning/sticking
3. Add in the leeks and carrot and spray again with the cooking oil spray and fry for a couple more minutes until the leeks have cooked down a little. Again added a little bit of the stock to prevent any burning/sticking
4. Stir in the thyme, Bay leaves (plus chilli flakes if using).
5. Add the potatoes and stock then bring to a boil.
6. Reduce heat and cover and simmer for approx 45 minutes.
7. Roughly blend some of the soup with a hand blender or you can add half of the soup to a traditional blender. I like to keep some chunks of vegetables in my soup but you can blend it all if you like a smooth soup.
8. Taste and season with salt and pepper as needed.
9. Sprinkle with fresh parsley.

Split Pea and Bacon Soup

 6 servings  1 hour 20 minutes

INGREDIENTS

- 250g (9oz) of lean thick bacon (or thick ham), chopped
- 150g (5.5oz) of celery, chopped
- 100g (3.5oz) of onion, chopped
- 200g (7oz) of carrots, chopped
- 3 cloves of garlic
- 300g (1.5 cups) of yellow split peas
- 5 cups (1.2 litres) of chicken or vegetable stock
- cooking oil spray
- salt and black pepper
- parsley - optional

DIRECTIONS

1. Spray a large pot with some spray oil over medium-high heat.
2. Add the bacon, and fry until browned, remove and set aside
3. Spray the pot with cooking oil spray again and add the onion, garlic, carrots, and celery and fry till softened.
4. Add the split peas and stock and bring to a boil, reduce heat, cover and simmer for approx 1 hour.
5. Add the bacon back in for the last 20 minutes of cooking time.
6. Soup is ready when peas have softened and soup is thickened.
7. Taste and season as needed with salt and black pepper.
8. Stir through some chopped fresh parsley (optional)

Turkey Taco Soup

 6 servings  55 minutes

INGREDIENTS

- 1lb (450g) of extra lean turkey mince
- 1 onion, diced
- 2 cloves of garlic, minced
- 250g (9oz) of fresh tomatoes, skinned and chopped
- 1 red pepper, diced
- 1 green pepper, diced
- 170g (1 cup) of frozen corn
- 400g (14oz) can of black beans, drained and rinsed
- 5 tablespoons of tomato paste (puree)
- 4 cups (960ml) of chicken stock - 3 cups (720ml) for Pressure cooker method
- spray oil
- salt and black pepper to taste

For the taco seasoning:

- 1 tablespoon of chilli powder (mild) - do not use pure Indian chilli powder.
- 2 teaspoons of granulated sweetener
- 1 teaspoon of sweet paprika
- 1 teaspoon of cumin
- ½ teaspoon of onion powder
- ½ teaspoon of garlic powder
- ½ teaspoon of oregano
- ¼ teaspoon of smoked paprika (this add a slightly smoky flavour)
- ¼ to ½ teaspoon of cayenne (omit if you don't like spicy)

DIRECTIONS

1. Mix taco seasoning ingredients together in a bowl
2. Spray a deep pot with spray oil over a medium high heat
3. Add the ground turkey, garlic and onion and fry till turkey is browned
4. Stir in the taco seasoning.
5. Add all other ingredients and mix well
6. Bring to a boil, then cover and simmer for approx 30-40 minutes.
7. Add a little additional water or stock if soup is too thick and season to taste with salt and black pepper.
8. Ladle into bowls and enjoy with your favourite topping.

Chicken Chickpea Spinach Soup

 4 servings  35 minutes

INGREDIENTS

- 1 tbs of olive oil
- 1 onion, diced
- 2 carrots, halved lengthways and sliced
- 3 garlic cloves, minced
- pinch of salt and black pepper
- 1 tsp of fennel seeds, crushed
- pinch of dried oregano
- 1.5 tsps of paprika
- 1 400g can of chickpeas (garbanzo beans), with the juice
- 2 tbs of tomato paste
- 4 cups of chicken or vegetable stock
- 250g of cooked chicken breast, diced
- 2 handfuls of chopped fresh spinach

DIRECTIONS

1. Add the olive oil to a deep saucepan over a medium-high heat
2. Once the oil is heated add in the onion, carrots and garlic and fry for a few minutes to soften
3. Add in the fennel, oregano and paprika and fry for another minute to coat.
4. Add in the chickpeas, tomato paste and stock, stir well and then bring to a boil.
5. Once it comes to a boil, reduce the heat to a simmer, add a lid and let simmer for 20 minutes.
6. Then add in the cooked chicken and spinach and stir until the spinach is all wilted down (a couple of minutes).
7. Taste and season as needed with salt and black pepper.

Chicken Noodle Soup

 4 servings  2 hours 15 minutes

INGREDIENTS

For the soup base:

- 1 Roast Chicken Carcass
- 1 onion, chopped
- 2 carrots, chopped
- 2 cloves of garlic, finely chopped
- 2 teaspoons of Italian Herbs
- salt and black pepper

For the soup:

- 1 onion, finely chopped
- 1 carrot, finely chopped
- 1 parsnip, finely chopped
- 90g/3oz of uncooked spaghetti, broken in half (can use gluten free pasta or use Spaghetti Squash, Spiralled Zucchini or another alternative to make this gluten free)
- some leftover cooked chicken (I saved some meat from the Roast Chicken)
- fresh Italian parsley
- salt and black pepper
- spray oil

DIRECTIONS

1. Spray a large pot with spray oil over a medium high heat, add the onion, carrots, garlic and Italian herbs and fry for a few mins to soften. Break up the chicken carcass and add to the pot.
2. Cover with 2 litres of water and season well with salt and black pepper. Bring to a boil and then reduce heat to low, cover and simmer for approx 1-1 ½ hours.
3. Drain the soup base over a sieve, so that you just have the liquid/stock and set aside.
4. Clean pot and spray with some low calorie spray, add the onion, carrots and parsnips and fry till softened and lightly golden. (I like to add a parsnip into my soup as I find it gives a lovely flavour)
5. Add in the homemade stock and bring to a boil, reduce heat to low, cover and simmer for about 1 hour, until veg is tender.
6. For the last 20 min of cooking time, add in the cooked chicken and spaghetti.
7. Season to taste with salt and black pepper and garnish with chopped Italian parsley.

Chicken Tortilla Soup

 4 servings  35 minutes

INGREDIENTS

- 1 tbs of olive oil
- 1 medium onion, diced
- 2-3 cloves of garlic, minced
- 1 x 4oz (113g) can of green chiles or use 1-2 chopped jalapenos, seeded
- 1 tbs cumin
- 1 tsp of paprika
- 1 tsp of Mexican Chili (Chilli) Powder
- ½ tsp of hot smoked paprika
- 1 x 400g (14oz) can of chopped tomatoes
- 1 cup (175g) of sweetcorn
- 2 tbs of tomato paste
- 2 cups (480ml) of chicken stock
- 300g (10.5oz) of leftover cooked chicken
- fresh chopped cilantro
- 55g (2oz) of crushed tortilla chips
- salt and black pepper to season

DIRECTIONS

1. Add the olive oil to a deep saucepan over a medium-high heat
2. Add the onion and fry for a couple of minutes to soften
3. Add the minced garlic and fry for a further 30 secs
4. Add in the diced green chiles (or jalapeno) and continue to fry for a minute.
5. Add in the cumin, Mexican chili powder, paprika and smoked paprika and stir to coat.
6. Add in the chopped tomatoes, corn, tomato paste and stock. Bring to a boil and then cover and simmer for 20 minutes.
7. Add in the cooked chicken and simmer until heated through.
8. Taste and season as needed with salt and black pepper.
9. Ladle into bowls and top with chopped cilantro and crushed tortilla chips.

Sweet Potato, Red Pepper and Carrot Soup

 4 servings  40 minutes

INGREDIENTS

- 1 large sweet potato, peeled and chopped (approx 350g)
- 1 large carrot, finely chopped
- 1 red bell pepper, finely chopped
- 2 cloves of garlic, crushed
- 1 medium onion, finely chopped
- 2 teaspoons of paprika
- 1.5 teaspoons of ground cumin
- 1 teaspoon of ground coriander
- ½ teaspoon of turmeric
- ½ teaspoon of cayenne pepper
- 960ml (4 cups) of chicken or vegetable stock
- Salt and pepper to season
- olive oil spray
- 1 large handful of freshly chopped coriander (optional)

DIRECTIONS

1. Spray a large deep saucepan over a medium high heat with olive oil spray
2. Add onion and carrot fry for a couple of minutes,
3. Add in the red pepper, sweet potato, garlic, paprika, cumin, coriander, turmeric and cayenne and stir well to coat
4. Add in the stock, Bring to a boil and then simmer for 20 minutes until all vegetables are softened
5. Add half the soup to a blender and blend until smooth and add this back into the soup and continue to simmer until your preferred thickness.
6. Season with salt and pepper to taste
7. Stir in the fresh coriander.

Coconut Chicken Rice Soup

 4 servings  35 minutes

INGREDIENTS

- 1 onion, diced
- 2 cloves of garlic, minced
- 1 tbs of grated fresh ginger root
- 1 tbs of medium curry powder
- pinch of red chilli flakes (optional)
- 400g can of chopped tomatoes
- ¾ cup (150g) of long grain rice (uncooked)
- 2.5 cups (600ml) of chicken stock
- 1.5 cups (approx 200g) of cooked chicken
- ½ cup (120ml) of coconut milk
- salt and black pepper
- chopped fresh coriander (cilantro)
- Cooking oil spray (I used Avocado)

DIRECTIONS

1. Spray a deep saucepan with some cooking oil spray over a medium-high heat.
2. Add the onion and fry for a few minutes to soften, you can add a little splash of water if needed to prevent any sticking.
3. Once the onion is softened add in the garlic, ginger, curry powder and chilli flakes fry for another minute. Again add a splash of water if needed so it doesn't stick.
4. Add in the chopped tomatoes, rice, stock and cooked chicken.
5. Bring to a boil and then simmer for about 15 minutes, until rice is cooked.
6. Add in the coconut milk and stir until creamy and heated through.
7. Taste and season as needed with salt and black pepper.
8. Stir in some chopped cilantro (coriander)

Poultry

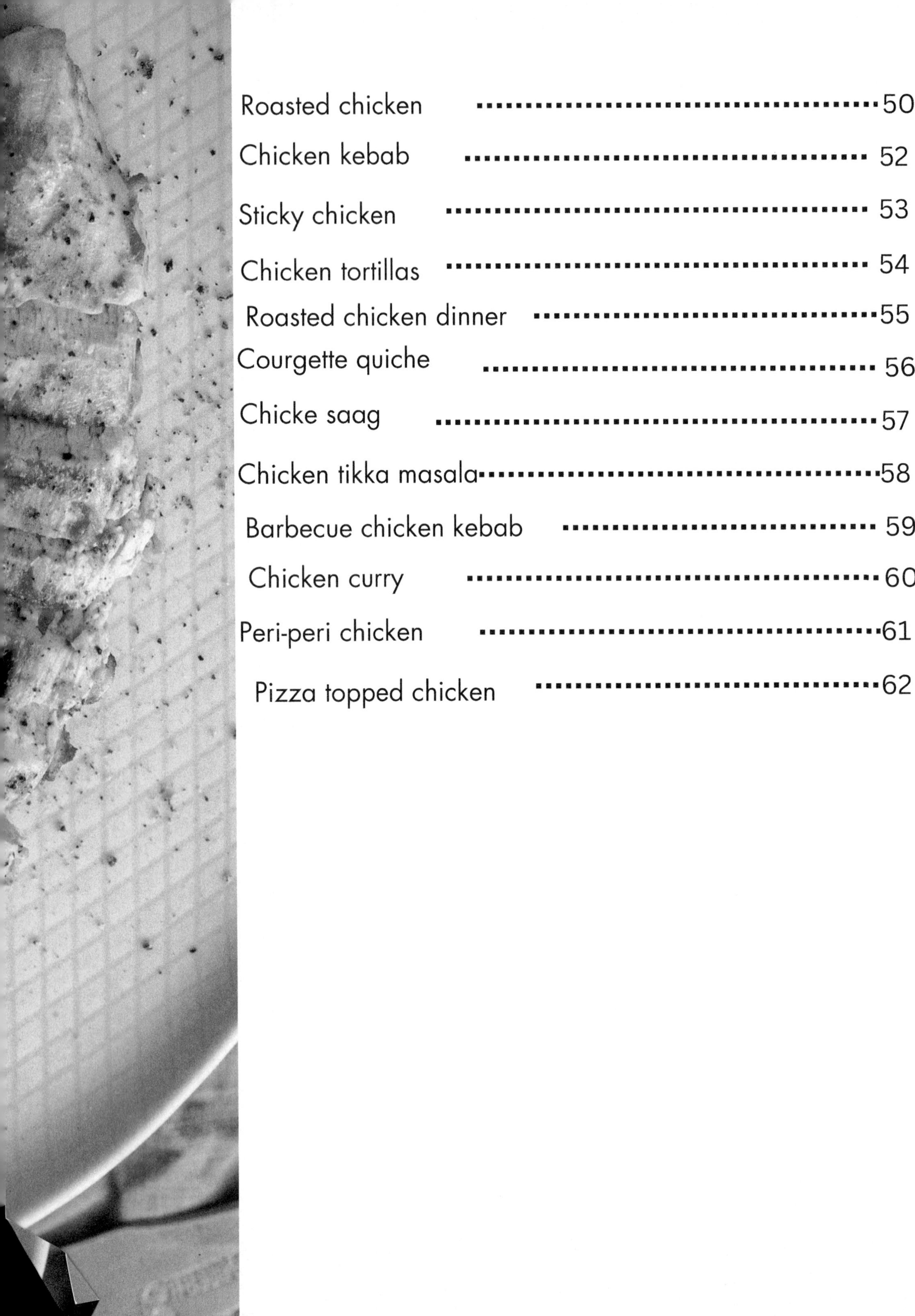

Roasted chicken 50

Chicken kebab 52

Sticky chicken 53

Chicken tortillas 54

Roasted chicken dinner 55

Courgette quiche 56

Chicke saag 57

Chicken tikka masala 58

Barbecue chicken kebab 59

Chicken curry 60

Peri-peri chicken 61

Pizza topped chicken 62

Roast chicken with yorkshire pudding

 4 servings  1 hour 20 minutes

INGREDIENTS

For the chicken-

- 1.5kg Chicken
- Slat & Pepper
- 1 tbsp Mustard Powder
- 1 tbsp Garlic Granules
- Fry Light

For Roast Potatoes

- Enough potatoes to fill you roasting tin
- Salt & Papper
- 1 pint of chicken stock, cubed is fine

For Gravy

- 1 large onion, finely diced
- salt & pepper
- 1/2 pint stock, 1/2 a pint of boiling water
- red wine vinegar

For Stuffing

- 1 mug of cous cous
- 1 chopped onion
- 1 tbsp sage
- Salt & Pepper
- 1 mug of stock

For Yorkshire

- 1 egg
- 1 tbsp flour
- 3 tbsp milk

DIRECTIONS

1. Pre-heat the oven to 190 degrees
2. Place the chicken on an oven proof dish and sprinkle with salt, pepper, mustard powder and garlic. Spray a small amount of fry light and cover the chicken with tin foil.
3. The chicken takes about an hour to cook, so the potatoes should be put in around 15 minutes into the chicken cooking
4. Leave the chicken to stand for 5 minutes before carving

For the roast potatoes

1. Peel the potatoes and chop to roast potato size
2. Par boil the potatoes for 5 minutes
3. Drain the water and shake the pan to fluff the potatoes up
4. Put potatoes on a roasting tin and pour the stock over the potatoes, ensuring they all get a covering. Fill no higher than half way up the potatoes.
5. Put them into the oven at 190 degrees. Make sure you bast them at least 3 times. You will know they're ready because there will be no stock left in the tray and the potatoes will be crispy

For the gravy-

1. Put all the ingredients in a small sauce pan and bring to the boil.
2. Simmer on a low heat for 10-15 minutes or until the onion is cooked
3. Allow to cool slightly and place in a blender, the onion should thicken the gravy

DIRECTIONS

For the stuffing:

1. Add the cous cous into a dish, add the onions, sage and seasoning
2. Add 1 mug of boiling water and leave to stand
3. Add 1 mug of stock and mix together, bake for 25 minutes

For the Yorkshire Pudding (2 syns per pudding):

1. Add all the ingredients to a bowl and mix into a batter, leave for at least 10 minutes before cooking
2. Add 1 spray of fry light into a muffing tin and put the tin in the oven for a few mins
3. Remove from the oven and add mixture into 2 muffin holes and cook for 25-30 mins, until risen and fluffy

Chicken kebab

 4 servings  20 minutes+1 hour marinating

INGREDIENTS

- 8 skinless and boneless chicken thighs, visible fat removed, cut into bite-size pieces
- 3 level tbsp tikka curry powder (see tip)
- 250g fat-free natural Greek-style yogurt
- 3 garlic cloves, crushed
- 4 x 60g wholemeal pitta breads
- Lemon wedges, to serve

For the salad:

- 1 cucumber, halved lengthways, deseeded and roughly chopped
- 200g radishes, trimmed and quartered
- 3 celery sticks, roughly chopped
- 2 little gem lettuces, shredded
- 100g fat-free natural Greek-style yogurt
- 25g fresh coriander, leaves roughly chopped, reserving a few whole sprigs for the kebabs

DIRECTIONS

1. Put the chicken in a freezer bag (or a glass or stainless-steel bowl) with the curry powder, yogurt and garlic. Season lightly with salt and stir to combine. Seal the bag or cover the bowl with cling film and marinate in the fridge for at least 1 hour or overnight if possible.
2. For the salad, put the cucumber, radishes, celery and lettuce in a bowl. Mix together the yogurt and chopped coriander, season to taste, then stir through the salad.
3. Preheat your grill to high. Lift the chicken out of the marinade, letting any excess drain off, then thread onto 4 metal skewers. Place the kebabs on a baking tray lined with foil and grill for 10-12 minutes, turning halfway, or until the chicken is lightly charred and cooked through.
4. Toast the pitta breads. Scatter the coriander sprigs over the chicken skewers and serve with the salad, 1 pitta per person and the lemon wedges for squeezing over.

Sticky chicken

 4 servings 30 minutes+ 30 minutes marinating

INGREDIENTS

- 3 level tbsp honey
- 3 tbsp balsamic vinegar
- 3 tbsp soy sauce/tamari
- 4 skinless and boneless chicken breasts, cut into chunks

DIRECTIONS

1. Mix together the honey, vinegar and soy sauce. Toss the chicken cubes in the mix to coat well, and leave to stand for at least 30 minutes in the fridge.
2. Heat a non-stick frying pan and add the chicken cubes and marinade. Cook on a medium-high heat for about 20 minutes, stirring frequently, until all the chicken has absorbed the liquid.
3. When the chicken is cooked through, serve with boiled plain rice and steamed pak choi.

Chicken and Black Bean Mini Tortillas

 12 servings  25 minutes

INGREDIENTS

- 1 pack Old El Paso Stand n Stuff Soft Mini Tortillas
- reduced fat cheddar grated. We used about 6g on each tortillas
- 2 chicken breast cut into strips
- 1 onion sliced
- 1 red pepper deseeded and sliced
- 1 yellow pepper deseeded and sliced
- 3 cloves garlic crushed
- 1 tin chopped tomatoes
- 1 tin black beans rinsed and drained
- 1/2 tsp chilli powder
- 1/4 tsp cayenne pepper
- 1 tsp cumin powder
- 1 tsp dried oregano
- 1/2 lemon juice only
- low calorie cooking spray
- sea salt to taste
- freshly ground black pepper to taste

DIRECTIONS

1. Heat up a large frying pan sprayed with some low calorie cooking spray.
2. Add the onions and crushed garlic, then cook until they just start to soften.
3. Add the chicken strips and peppers and cook until the chicken starts to colour.
4. Mix in all the spices and lemon juice.
5. Continue to cook for a minute or so.
6. Add the chopped tomatoes and drained black beans, then season to taste. This will take a fair amount of seasoning so add a good pinch. You can adjust the seasoning more later.
7. Cover the pan, allow the mix to cook simmer for 10 minutes. There isn't much liquid in this recipe (it would get messy if it was too wet!) so keep an eye on it.
8. Check the chicken is cooked through, check the seasoning (add some more if you want) then spoon the mix into the Old El Paso Stand n Stuff Soft Mini Tortillas.
9. Sprinkle the grated cheese over the top of each one and pop in the oven for 5 minutes at 200°C or until the cheese has melted.
10. Remove from the oven and enjoy! But be careful they will be very hot!!

Roast chicken dinner

 2 servings  30 minutes

INGREDIENTS

- 2 large fresh thyme sprigs
- 2 skinless and boneless chicken breasts
- 4 bacon medallions, visible fat removed
- 2 Slimming World Free Food Pork Sausages (available from Iceland stores), thawed slightly and halved
- 200g Chantenay carrots, halved or quartered lengthways if large (baby carrots or carrot batons work well too)
- Low-calorie cooking spray
- 560g can new potatoes, drained, halved if large
- 150g broccoli florets, halved if large
- 125g frozen peas
- 1 chicken stock pot
- Chopped fresh parsley, to serve

DIRECTIONS

1. Preheat your oven to 220°C/fan 200°C/gas 7 and put the thyme sprigs in a non-stick roasting tin.
2. Make a few deep cuts in each chicken breast, taking care not to cut all the way through (this will help them cook faster), and place on top of the thyme. Wrap a bacon medallion around each sausage piece and add these to the tin too, along with the carrots. Spray with low-calorie cooking spray and roast for 5 minutes.
3. Add the potatoes and broccoli to the tin, taking care not to crowd the chicken and sausages, and roast for another 10 minutes.
4. Meanwhile, put the peas in a heatproof bowl, cover with boiling water and leave to stand for 5 minutes. Drain well, scatter around the roasting tin and return to the oven for another 10 minutes or until everything is cooked through.
5. Put the stock pot and 200ml boiling water in a heatproof jug and whisk to make a quick gravy.
6. Discard the thyme and pour the gravy over everything. Scatter over the parsley and serve hot.

Spiralized Courgette Quiche

 6 servings 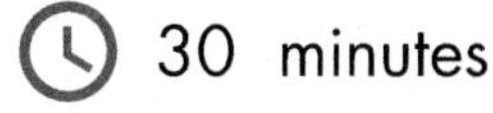 30 minutes

INGREDIENTS

- 1 large courgette
- 1 red pepper sliced
- 9 slices tomato
- 8 large eggs
- 2 tbsp quark
- 2 spring onions chopped
- 1 handful fresh parsley chopped
- sea salt
- freshly ground black pepper

DIRECTIONS

1. Preheat the oven to 190°C.
2. Spiralize the courgette using the linguine cutting cone, then sprinkle with a little sea salt.
3. In a bowl, mix the eggs and quark together and season.
4. Place the courgette, spring onion, peppers and parsley in the quiche dish.
5. Pour in the eggs mixture.
6. Place the sliced tomato on top, season with a little salt and black pepper.
7. Cook for 20-25 minutes or until the quiche is set and starting to colour.
8. Allow to cool slightly before removing the quiche from the dish and serving.

Chicken Saag

 2 servings  50 minutes

INGREDIENTS

- Low-calorie cooking spray
- 2 medium onions, finely chopped
- 200g closed-cup mushrooms, sliced
- 6cm piece of root ginger, peeled and finely chopped
- 3 large garlic cloves, finely chopped
- 2 tbsp medium curry powder*
- 3 tbsp tomato purée
- 1 chicken stock cube
- 700g skinless and boneless chicken breasts, cut into bite-sized chunks
- 1 ripe tomato, roughly chopped
- 100g baby leaf spinach, roughly chopped
- Large handful of roughly chopped fresh coriander
- 4tbsp fat-free natural Greek yogurt

DIRECTIONS

1. Spray a large, deep non-stick frying pan with low-calorie cooking spray and place over a medium heat.
2. Add the onions and fry for 5 minutes, adding a little water if they start to stick.
3. Add the mushrooms, ginger and garlic and cook for a further 5 minutes.
4. Stir in the curry powder, tomato purée, stock cube and 300ml of water and cook for 2 minutes.
5. Add the chicken and simmer for 10 minutes.
6. Add the tomato, spinach and coriander and cook for a further 5 minutes or until the chicken is cooked through.
7. Take the pan off the heat, stir the yogurt into the curry and season lightly. Serve hot with rice and your favourite vegetables.

Chicken tikka masala

 4 servings  1 hour+ 3 hours marinating

INGREDIENTS

- 160g fat-free natural yogurt
- Seeds from 6 cardamom pods, crushed
- Juice of 1 lime, plus wedges to serve
- 6 garlic cloves, crushed
- 6cm piece fresh root ginger, peeled and grated
- 4 tbsp tikka curry powder*
- 8 large skinless and boneless chicken thighs, visible fat removed, cut into large chunks
- Low-calorie cooking spray
- 1 large onion, finely chopped
- 500g passata
- 4 tbsp chopped fresh coriander, plus extra to serve

DIRECTIONS

1. Put 100g yogurt in a large bowl and stir in the cardamom, lime juice, half the garlic, half the ginger and half the tikka powder. Add the chicken and toss well, then cover and chill for 3-4 hours, or overnight if possible (if you're in a hurry, 30 minutes is better than nothing!).
2. Spray a wide non-stick saucepan with low-calorie cooking spray and put it over a medium-low heat. Add the onion and the rest of the garlic and ginger, then cover and simmer for 15 minutes, stirring occasionally.
3. Add the passata, coriander and remaining tikka powder and bring to the boil. Reduce the heat slightly and simmer briskly for 20-30 minutes or until the sauce has thickened.
4. At the same time, preheat your grill to high and line a baking tray with foil. Arrange the chicken chunks on the tray and grill for 15 minutes or until cooked through, turning occasionally.
5. Blitz the sauce until smooth with a stick blender (or use a food processor and return to the pan). Bring back to a simmer, then season to taste, remove from the heat and stir in the rest of the yogurt. Stir the chicken chunks into the sauce and serve with lime wedges, rice (we cooked ours with a little ground turmeric and stirred through some chopped chilli), Speed veg or salad and with the extra coriander scattered over.

Barbecue chicken kebab

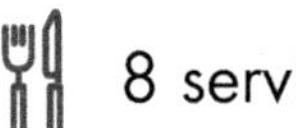

8 servings

2 hours 40 minutes

INGREDIENTS

- 12 boneless, skinless chicken thighs
- 500g Greek yogurt
- 2 lemons, juiced, ½ lemon zested
- 100ml olive oil
- 4 garlic cloves, very finely grated or crushed
- 1 tbsp ground coriander
- 1 tbsp ground cumin
- 1 tbsp sweet paprika
- 1 tsp dried oregano
- 1 tsp dried thyme
- 1 tsp cayenne pepper
- 1 tsp crushed black pepper
- ½ tsp ground cinnamon
- 2 red onions, halved and finely sliced
- 4 tomatoes (plum work well) halved and sliced

DIRECTIONS

1. First, whisk all the marinade ingredients together with 1 tsp salt in a large bowl or, better still, a large plastic container that has a lid. Open out each chicken thigh, cover with a piece of baking parchment and flatten it with your hand, then lift off the paper and cut the thigh in half. Tip into the marinade and mix so it's completely coated. Cover, chill and marinate for at least 1 hr or up to 24 hrs – the longer, the better.
2. Thread all the chicken onto two skewers so that both skewers go through each piece of meat, packing down tightly as you go to make a compact kebab.
3. Light a lidded barbecue , and let the flames die down. Once the coals have turned ashen, pile them up on one side with a single layer of coals scattered around the other side. Lay the chicken kebab on the side of the barbecue with only a few coals underneath. Put the lid down and cook for 45 mins, turning every 15 mins. To finish, lift the lid and roll the kebab over to the hotter side to char the meat, turning it every few minutes until well browned and cooked through. Prise the chicken pieces apart in the centre to check they're cooked, or use a digital cooking thermometer – it should read 70C or more. Leave to rest for 5-10 mins while you cook the pittas (see recipe, opposite). Bring the kebab to the table and carve into thin slices with a serrated knife. Pile the carved meat into the warm pittas, then the sliced red onions and tomatoes, chips and tzatziki (see our recipes, below).

Chicken curry

 4 servings  1 hour 10 minutes

INGREDIENTS

- 2 large onions, diced
- 600ml hot chicken stock
- 4 cloves
- 1 tsp ground cumin
- 1 tsp ground coriander
- 1 x 2½cm piece cinnamon stick
- 3 cardamom pods
- ½ tsp mild chilli powder
- 2 tsp ground turmeric
- 4 black peppercorns
- 1 tbsp peeled and grated fresh root ginger
- 3 garlic cloves, crushed
- 4 skinless and boneless chicken breasts, cut into chunks
- 275ml fat-free natural yogurt, plus extra to serve
- 2 tbsp chopped coriander leaves, to serve

DIRECTIONS

1. Put the onions and 425ml chicken stock in a large, heavy-based non-stick saucepan. Cover the pan, bring to the boil and then boil for 10 minutes. Reduce the heat, uncover the pan and cook gently for 20 minutes, until the onion is tender.
2. Add all the spices, fresh ginger and garlic to the pan, and cook for 3-4 minutes. Tip in the chicken chunks and cook for a few minutes to coat in the spices, then stir in the remaining chicken stock.
3. Cover the pan and simmer very gently for 20 minutes, or until the chicken is cooked through.
4. Transfer the curry to a large serving bowl. Add 4 tbsp of the cooking sauce to the yogurt and stir well. Gradually add the yogurt to the curry, stirring continuously. Remove the cloves and cinnamon stick.
5. Season to taste, sprinkle with the coriander and serve with boiled plain rice, Speed veg and the extra yogurt for spooning over.

Piri-piri chicken with spiced wedges

INGREDIENTS

- 350g pot Slimming World Creamy Tomato Sauce
- 1kg chicken drumsticks
- 1 red chilli, deseeded and finely chopped
- 1 garlic clove, crushed
- 1 tsp dried oregano
- 4 tsp paprika
- 2 skinless and boneless chicken breasts, halved diagonally
- 4 baking potatoes, cut into wedges
- Low-calorie cooking spray
- 2 tbsp roughly chopped fresh parsley
- Grated zest and juice of 1 unwaxed lemon, plus wedges to serve

DIRECTIONS

1. Preheat your oven to 200°C/fan 180°C/gas 6.
2. Cook the tomato sauce according to the pot instructions.
3. While the sauce is cooking, skin the drumsticks by picking away the skin at the thicker end and pulling it off over the bony end, using kitchen paper to get a good grip. Slash each of the drumsticks a couple of times at the thick end, getting right down to the bone.
4. Pour half of the tomato sauce into a large mixing bowl (and keep the rest of the sauce warm, if possible) and stir in the chilli, garlic, oregano and 3 tsp paprika. Lightly season the chicken drumsticks and breasts, add to the mixing bowl and toss to coat well. Transfer all the chicken to a large non-stick roasting tin and cook for 40 minutes or until lightly charred and cooked through.
5. Put the potatoes in another non-stick roasting tin, sprinkle with the remaining paprika and season lightly. Spray with low-calorie cooking spray, toss well and roast above the chicken for 35 minutes or until golden and cooked, turning once. Scatter over the parsley.
6. Pile the chicken onto a large platter, scatter over the lemon zest and sprinkle over the juice. Serve with the potato wedges, lemon wedges, the rest of the hot tomato sauce and a big salad.

Pizza-topped chicken

 1 serving 

INGREDIENTS

- ½ small red onion, finely chopped
- ½ red pepper, deseeded and chopped
- 1 small garlic clove, crushed
- Low-calorie cooking spray
- 2 on-the-vine tomatoes, skinned and chopped
- 1 tbsp canned chopped tomatoes
- 1 tsp tomato purée
- 1 tsp dried oregano
- 1 skinless and boneless chicken breast
- 40g reduced-fat Cheddar, grated
- 1 cherry tomato, halved
- 1 tsp finely chopped fresh basil

DIRECTIONS

1. Put the onion, pepper and garlic in a small non-stick saucepan sprayed with low-calorie cooking spray and cook for a few minutes until softened. Stir in the fresh tomatoes, canned tomatoes, tomato purée and oregano and simmer for 5 minutes. Set aside.
2. Preheat your oven to 220°C/fan 200°C/gas 7.
3. Cut the chicken breast in half horizontally, being careful not to cut it all the way through. Fold it open to create a butterfly shape.
4. Spray a non-stick frying pan with low-calorie cooking spray and put it over a medium heat. Add the chicken and cook until browned on both sides. Put the chicken on a non-stick baking tray and bake for 15-20 minutes or until cooked through.
5. Remove the chicken from the oven and spread the tomato mixture on top. Sprinkle over the cheese and put the cherry tomato on top. Cook for a further 5 minutes, until the cheese melts.
6. Sprinkle with the basil and serve hot, with Slimming World chips and a huge crispy salad.

Beef, Pork & Lamb

Chilli con carne 65
Roasted pork & veg 66
Steak pie 67
Sticky roast pork 68
Cheeseburger quiche 69
Sausage tray bake 70
Pomegranate brisket 71
Donner kebab 72
Beef kofta kebab 73
Chilli crispy beef 74
Braised steak & root veg mash 75
Chiptole steak & sweet potto chips 76
Beef curry 77
Beef hotpot bake 78
Beef stroganoff 79
Cottage pie 80
Chilli with rice 81
Cowboy hotpot 82
Scotch eggs 83
Toad in the hole 84
Bbq pulled pork 85
Lancashire hotpot 86

Chilli con carne

 4 serving  55 minutes

INGREDIENTS

- Low-calorie cooking spray
- 500g lean beef mince (5% fat or less)
- 1 large onion, finely chopped
- 2 large red peppers, deseeded and diced
- 3 garlic cloves, finely chopped
- 1 red chilli, deseeded and chopped
- 1 heaped tbsp tomato purée
- 1 tbsp dried oregano
- 1 tbsp smoked paprika
- 1 tbsp ground cumin
- 1 tsp chilli powder
- 400g can red kidney beans, drained and rinsed
- 2 x 400g cans chopped tomatoes
- 1 beef stock cube, crumbled
- 300g dried long-grain rice
- 1 tsp ground turmeric
- ½ small pack fresh coriander, chopped

DIRECTIONS

1. Spray a large non-stick saucepan with low-calorie cooking spray and place over a high heat. Add the beef and cook for 5 minutes, breaking up any lumps with a spoon, then drain off any fat.
2. Add the onion, peppers, garlic, chopped chilli, tomato purée, oregano, paprika, cumin and chilli powder to the pan, then reduce the heat to medium and cook for 5 minutes.
3. Add the beans, chopped tomatoes, stock cube and 300ml boiling water to the pan. Bring back to the boil over a high heat, then reduce the heat to low and simmer for 30 minutes.
4. Meanwhile, put the rice and turmeric in a pan and cook according to the pack instructions. Drain well and stir in the coriander.
5. Serve the chilli with your favourite Speed veg or salad.

Roast pork with one-pan vegetables

 4 serving  1 hour 40 minutes

INGREDIENTS

- 1 tbsp vegetable stock
- 1 tsp mustard powder
- Juice and zest of 1 unwaxed lemon
- 900g boneless pork loin, visible fat removed
- 800g floury potatoes, such as Maris Piper or King Edward, quartered
- 2 medium leeks, roughly chopped
- 1 medium red onion, cut into wedges
- 1 medium butternut squash, peeled, deseeded and cut into 2.5cm cubes
- 3 parsnips, cut into 2.5cm cubes
- Low-calorie cooking spray
- 2 tsp dried thyme
- Handful fresh thyme leaves, roughly chopped

DIRECTIONS

1. Preheat your oven to 190°C/fan 170°C/gas 5. Mix together the stock, mustard and lemon juice and zest.
2. Line a roasting tin with foil and put the pork in the tin. Brush the mustard mixture over the meat, making sure you cover the sides.
3. In a separate non-stick roasting tin, spread out the potatoes, leeks, red onion, squash and parsnips. Spray with low-calorie cooking spray, sprinkle over the dried thyme and 1 tbsp water.
4. Put the pork on the top shelf of the oven and the vegetables on the next shelf below and cook for 1 hour, or until cooked through.
5. Remove the pork from the oven and leave to rest for 15 minutes. Meanwhile, move the vegetables to the top shelf and cook for a further 10 minutes, until golden.
6. Tip the vegetables onto a large serving platter and season lightly. Slice the pork on a board, then pile it on top of the vegetables. Serve hot, with the fresh thyme and some freshly ground black pepper sprinkled over.

Steak pie

 4 serving  1 hour 10 minutes

INGREDIENTS

- Low-calorie cooking spray
- 600g beef frying steaks, visible fat removed, cut into bite-size pieces
- 400g chestnut mushrooms, quartered
- 2 carrots, cut into small cubes
- 200g swede, peeled and cut into small cubes
- 2 onions, finely chopped
- 2 garlic cloves, finely chopped
- 1 tsp dried mixed herbs
- 2 tbsp Worcestershire sauce
- 400ml hot beef stock
- 1 level tbsp gravy granules
- 100g puff pastry
- 1 egg, beaten
- 400g kale, shredded

DIRECTIONS

1. Preheat your oven to 220°C/fan 200°C/gas 7. Spray a large, heavy-based non-stick pan with low-calorie cooking spray and put it over a high heat. Add the steak and stir-fry for 5-6 minutes, or until browned all over.
2. Add the mushrooms, carrots, swede, onions, garlic, herbs, Worcestershire sauce, stock and gravy granules and bring to the boil. Reduce the heat and simmer gently for 12-15 minutes, or until the sauce has thickened. Divide the steak filling between 4 individual pie dishes.
3. Roll out the pastry on baking paper and cut out 4 lids. Brush the rim of each dish with a little egg and top with a pastry lid, pressing down the edges to seal. Make a hole in the centre of each lid and brush with more egg.
4. Bake the pies for 15-20 minutes, or until risen and golden. Steam the kale for 4-5 minutes, or until just tender. Serve with the pies.

Sticky roast pork

 2 servings 

INGREDIENTS

- 500g frozen butternut squash chunks (or ½ large squash, if you want to prepare it yourself)
- 1 large red pepper, deseeded and cut into chunks
- 1 large red onion, roughly chopped
- 1 tsp garlic granules
- Low-calorie cooking spray
- 2 tbsp tomato purée
- 2 level tbsp mango chutney
- 1 lean pork tenderloin (about 300-400g), visible fat removed
- Small bag of watercress, to serve
- Fat-free natural Greek yogurt sprinkled with black pepper, to serve

DIRECTIONS

1. Preheat your oven to 200°C/fan 180°C/gas 6.
2. Put the squash, red pepper and onion in a medium-size non-stick roasting tin or ovenproof dish, sprinkle over the garlic granules and spray with low-calorie cooking spray.
3. In a small bowl, mix together the tomato purée and mango chutney. Brush this mixture all over the pork, then sit the pork on top of the vegetables and roast for 30-35 minutes or until the pork's cooked.
4. Take the tin out of the oven and set the pork aside on a plate to rest, loosely covered with foil. Return the veg to the oven for 5-10 minutes or until lightly charred. Slice the pork and return to the tin. Scatter over the watercress and serve with a drizzle of yogurt.

Cheeseburger Quiche

4 servings 55 minutes

INGREDIENTS

- 350g (12.5oz) of extra lean beef mince
- ½ tsp of sea salt
- ¾ cup (180ml) of crushed tomatoes (or use passata)
- 2 tablespoons of tomato paste (puree) - use 3 to 4 tablespoons if using passata
- 1 tablespoon of granulated sweetener
- ½ teaspoon of onion powder
- ½ teaspoon of garlic powder
- 1 teaspoon of paprika
- salt and black pepper
- 1 teaspoon of Worcestershire sauce
- 1 large onion, sliced
- 1 cup (225g) of fat-free cottage cheese
- 4 large eggs
- 120g (4oz) of cheddar cheese or Red Leicester(4xHEa's)
- Cooking oil spray

DIRECTIONS

1. Preheat oven to 200c or 400f (gas mark 6)
2. In a large bowl, add the beef mince and sea salt salt and mix together to combine.
3. Grease a quiche dish with some spray oil and add the meat mixture to the dish, flatten down well so it covers the bottom of the dish in a thin layer.
4. Place in the oven and bake for about 10 mins until lightly browned. The meat mixture will shrink on the base when cooked, but don't worry, as you will be covering it with more layers. Dab up any excess juices that are released with some kitchen towel. Set aside.
5. Spray a frying pan with some spray oil, add the onions and fry until golden and softened.
6. Mix the crushed tomatoes, garlic powder, onion powder, sweetener, salt, pepper, paprika, tomato paste and Worcestershire sauce together in a bowl.
7. Add the cottage cheese, eggs and a ⅓ of the cheddar to a blender and blend until smooth.
8. Now you can start layering the next layers.
9. Using a spatula, spread the tomato mixture over the meat layer.
10. Add the softened onions
11. Then pour in the cottage cheese mixture
12. Sprinkle over the top with the remaining cheddar
13. Then place back in the oven and bake until mixture is set and cheese is melted and lightly golden on top (approx 30 mins)

Sausage tray bake

 4 serving  1 hour 30 minutes

INGREDIENTS

- Low-calorie cooking spray
- 12 Slimming World Pork Sausages, halved (available from Iceland)
- 2 large onions, chopped
- 1 bay leaf
- 6 fresh thyme sprigs, leaves picked
- 5 fresh sage leaves, chopped
- 1 tbsp tomato purée
- 2 garlic cloves, chopped
- 1 chicken stock cube, crumbled
- 1 tbsp Bovril
- 1 tsp Worcestershire sauce
- 300g baby new potatoes, halved or quartered if large
- 2 carrots, chopped into chunks
- 3 red onions, sliced
- 1 small butternut squash, peeled, deseeded and chopped into chunks
- 3 portobello mushrooms, each cut into 6 pieces
- 4 fresh rosemary sprigs, each cut into 3 pieces

DIRECTIONS

1. Spray a non-stick saucepan with low-calorie cooking spray and put it over a high heat. Add the sausages and brown on all sides, then transfer to an ovenproof dish and set aside.
2. To make the sauce, add the chopped onions to the saucepan and cook for 5 minutes, until browned and softened, adding a splash of water if they stick. Add the bay leaf, thyme, sage, tomato purée, garlic, stock cube, Bovril, Worcestershire sauce and 1 litre boiling water and bring to the boil. Reduce to a simmer and cook for 15 minutes.
3. At the same time, bring another large saucepan of water to the boil over a high heat. Add the potatoes and carrots, reduce to a simmer and cook for 10 minutes. Drain well and add to the sausages in the dish.
4. Discard the bay leaf and blitz the sauce until smooth, either with a stick blender or in your food processor. Return the sauce to the pan if you used a food processor, add the sliced red onions and simmer for 15 minutes or until reduced by one-third.
5. Preheat your oven to 200°C/fan 180°C/gas 6.
6. Add the squash and mushrooms to the ovenproof dish and pour over the sauce. Top with the rosemary sprigs and roast for 30 minutes or until everything is cooked and tender.

Pomegranate brisket

 1 serving  30 minutes

INGREDIENTS

- beef brisket (if rolled, unroll it)
- red onions, finely sliced
- ½ pomegranate, seeds only
- cooked giant couscous tossed through with 10g coriander leaves, a little urfa chilli, sliced cucumber and lemon zest (optional), to serve
- 120ml pomegranate molasses
- 60ml olive oil
- 2 tsp ras el hanout
- 4 garlic cloves, finely chopped
- 1 tsp urfa chilli flakes

DIRECTIONS

1. Mix the marinade ingredients in a small bowl with ¾ tsp fine salt. Put the beef in a large, ovenproof dish. Pour half the marinade over the beef and spread evenly, then turn it over and pour the rest over the meat over the meat to coat. Cover and chill overnight.
2. Remove the meat from the fridge up to 1 hr before cooking to come up to room temperature. If it's a hot day, you can reduce that to 30 mins. Heat the oven to 240C/220C fan/gas 9.
3. Turn the meat in the marinade to make sure it is well coated, leaving the fatty layer on the top. Put half the sliced onions underneath the meat and spread the rest over the top. Cover the dish loosely with foil, making sure it is properly covered.
4. Roast for 15 mins, then turn the oven down to 170C/150C fan/gas 3 and cook for a further 2 hrs 30 mins-3 hrs. Check it to see how tender it is – a fork should go in and come out easily and the meat should flake well, if not, put back in the oven for another 30 mins.
5. Rest the brisket for 15 mins, still covered with foil, then transfer to a board. Decorate with the pomegranate seeds. Serve with the giant couscous, if you like, or shred with two forks, then spoon over some of the pomegranate sauce, then serve with pitta bread and dips of your choice.

Donner kebab

 4 serving 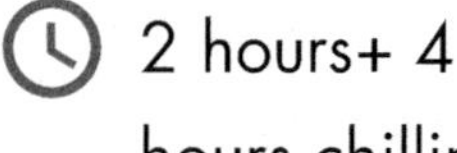 2 hours+ 4 hours chilling

INGREDIENTS

- Low-calorie cooking spray
- 1 onion, finely chopped
- 3 garlic cloves, crushed
- 500g lean beef mince (5% fat or less)
- ½ tsp ground ginger
- 1 tsp ground cumin
- ¼ tsp ground cinnamon
- 1 tsp paprika
- 1 egg, lightly beaten
- 1 tbsp dried mixed herbs or dried parsley
- 4 x 60g wholemeal pitta breads
- ½ iceberg lettuce, leaves shredded
- ½ red onion, sliced
- 4 tomatoes, sliced
- 4 large gherkins, drained and sliced
- For the dressing:
- 1 small garlic clove, crushed
- 200g fat-free-natural Greek yogurt

DIRECTIONS

1. Spray a large, heavy-based non-stick saucepan with low-calorie cooking spray and put it over a low heat. Add the onion and cook for 12-15 minutes, stirring occasionally, until softened and lightly browned.
2. Transfer the onion to your food processor and add the garlic, beef, ginger, cumin, cinnamon, paprika, egg and dried herbs. Season lightly and blend until fairly smooth. Turn out into a bowl.
3. Spoon the mixture into a non-stick loaf tin (it should fill to a little over halfway up the tin) and pat down. Cover and chill for 4 hours, or overnight if there's time.
4. When you're ready to cook, preheat your oven to 180°C/fan 160°C/gas 4.
5. Cover the loaf tin with foil and bake for 1 hour 20 minutes. Remove from the oven and drain off any liquid, then return to the oven, uncovered, for 10-12 minutes. Leave the tin to rest for 12-15 minutes, then remove the doner meat and slice thinly.
6. Lightly toast and open up the pittas, then stir the garlic into the yogurt for the dressing.
7. Fill each pitta with the meat and some lettuce, red onion, tomatoes and gherkins. Serve 1 pitta per person with the remaining salad and yogurt dressing. Add a twist of black pepper to serve.

Beef kofta kebab

 Makes 8 

INGREDIENTS

- 1 tsp cumin
- ½ tsp paprika
- ½ tsp turmeric
- ½ tsp cinnamon
- ½ tsp cayenne pepper
- 2 tsp garam masala
- 500g lean beef mince (5% fat or less)
- 1 medium onion, finely chopped
- 2 garlic cloves, finely chopped
- For the chilli sauce:
- 5 medium green chillies, deseeded
- ¼ tsp ground white pepper
- 1 garlic clove, peeled
- 1 tsp white wine vinegar
- Small handful of baby spinach leaves
- For the yogurt dressing:
- 6 tbsp fat-free natural Greek yogurt
- 1 tsp lemon juice
- ¼ tsp ground white pepper
- 1 small red chilli, deseeded and finely chopped

DIRECTIONS

1. Preheat your oven to 200°C/fan 180°C/gas 6.
2. To make the koftas, put all the spices in a large bowl, add ½ tsp each of salt and black pepper and mix well. Add the beef, onion and garlic and mix well with your hands. Divide the mixture into 8 equal portions and shape each portion into a sausage about 10cm long. Put the koftas in a baking tray and cook in the middle of the oven for 30 minutes, turning halfway.
3. Meanwhile, put the chill sauce ingredients in a small food processor or blender, season to taste with salt and blitz to a paste. Chill until needed.
4. Put all the ingredients for the yogurt dressing in a small bowl, season to taste with salt and mix well. Chill until needed.
5. Arrange the koftas on a serving dish, drizzle with the chilli sauce and yogurt dressing and serve hot with couscous and salad.

Crispy chilli beef

 4 servings  1 hour 5 minute

INGREDIENTS

- 1 medium egg
- 2 level tbsp cornflour
- 1 level tsp bicarbonate of soda
- 500g lean beef frying steak, visible fat removed, cut into thin strips
- Low-calorie cooking spray
- For the stir-fry:
- 4 level tbsp brown sauce
- 3 tbsp dark soy sauce
- 2 tbsp rice vinegar
- 4 garlic cloves, crushed
- 5cm-piece fresh root ginger, peeled and grated
- 3 tbsp orange and pineapple no-added-sugar squash diluted with 400ml water
- 2 tbsp Worcestershire sauce
- 2 tbsp tomato purée
- ½ tsp dried red chilli flakes
- 1 beef stock cube, crumbled
- 2 onions, thickly sliced
- 2 red peppers, deseeded and thickly sliced
- 200g carrots, cut into matchsticks
- 150g baby sweetcorn, halved lengthways
- 50g bean sprouts, rinsed
- 250g dried medium egg noodles
- Sliced red chilli, to serve

DIRECTIONS

1. Preheat your oven to 220°C/fan 200°C/gas 7.
2. Beat the egg with a fork, then stir in the cornflour and bicarbonate of soda until combined and season lightly. Toss the beef in the egg, then spread out on a large non-stick baking tray in a single layer and spray with low-calorie cooking spray. Cook for 30-40 minutes, until dark and crispy, turning halfway. Reduce the oven to its lowest setting and leave the beef inside while you make the rest of the dish.
3. Make the sauce by mixing together the brown sauce, soy sauce, vinegar, garlic, ginger, squash, Worcestershire sauce, tomato purée, chilli flakes and stock cube. Set aside.
4. Spray a large, non-stick wok or frying pan with low-calorie cooking spray and place over a medium-high heat. Add the onions, peppers and carrots, and stir-fry for 7-8 minutes until starting to soften. Add the sauce and corn. Increase the heat and simmer for 5-6 minutes, stirring often, until the sauce is reduced and syrupy, and the vegetables are just soft.
5. Add the beef to the stir-fry with the bean sprouts and bring back to a simmer. Cook the noodles according to the pack instructions, then drain. Divide the noodles and beef mixture between 4 bowls, and scatter over the chilli to serve.

Braised steak and root veg mash

 4 servings  3 hours 10 minutes

INGREDIENTS

- Low-calorie cooking spray
- 2 celery sticks, chopped
- 250g closed-cup mushrooms, chopped
- 3 garlic cloves, peeled
- 3 medium onions, cut into bite-size chunks
- 750g topside of beef, visible fat removed, cut into bite-size chunks
- 1 beef stock cube, crumbled
- 1 heaped tsp dried thyme
- 1 tbsp tomato purée
- 2 tsp Marmite
- 1½ tbsp Worcestershire sauce
- 1 large potato, peeled and cut into bite-size chunks
- 1 small carrot, finely chopped

For the mash

- 1 large potato, peeled and roughly chopped
- 1 small swede, peeled and roughly chopped
- 4 large carrots, peeled and roughly chopped

DIRECTIONS

1. Preheat the oven to 180 °C/ fan 160 °C/gas 4.
2. Spray a non-stick casserole pan with low-calorie cooking spray and place over a medium heat. Add the celery, mushrooms, garlic and half of the onions and fry for 10 minutes or until slightly caramelised, adding a little water if anything is sticking.
3. Meanwhile, spray a non-stick frying pan with low-calorie cooking spray and place over a high heat. Fry the beef in batches until browned all over and set aside.
4. Add the stock cube, thyme, tomato purée, Marmite and Worcestershire sauce to the veg in the casserole pan. Remove from the heat, stir in 800ml boiling water and purée using a stick blender (or use a liquidiser and return to the pan). Add the beef, potato chunks, finely chopped carrot and remaining onion and bring to the boil over a high heat. Cover and cook in the oven for 1 hour 15 minutes or until the meat is tender, stirring occasionally.
5. Meanwhile make the mash. Put the potato, swede and carrots in a saucepan of boiling water over a high heat and cook for 45 minutes or until very tender. Drain, mash and season lightly.
6. Check the seasoning of the beef and serve hot with the mash.

Chipotle steak with sweet potato chips

 1 serving  45 minutes

INGREDIENTS

- 1 large sweet potato, peeled and cut into chips
- Low-calorie cooking spray
- 1 small red pepper, deseeded and cut into wedges
- 8 baby sweetcorn
- Large pinch of chipotle chilli powder or flakes (see tip)
- Large pinch of paprika
- Pinch of garlic salt
- 1 lean beef steak, such as fillet or sirloin, visible fat removed
- Juice of ½ lime, plus a wedge to serve
- Small handful of fresh coriander, roughly chopped

DIRECTIONS

1. Boil the sweet potato chips for 5-6 minutes, or until just tender. Drain well and tip into a bowl, then toss with a little seasoning and spray with low-calorie cooking spray.
2. Put the red pepper and sweetcorn in another bowl, spray with low-calorie cooking spray and set aside.
3. Mix the chipotle powder, paprika and garlic salt in a small bowl. Spray the steak on both sides with low-calorie cooking spray and rub with the chipotle mixture to coat.
4. Place a large non-stick griddle pan over a high heat. When smoking hot, add the steak, red pepper and sweetcorn and cook for 2 minutes. Turn the steak and peppers over and shake the pan to move the sweetcorn.
5. Add the sweet potato chips and cook for a further 2-3 minutes, turning the vegetables frequently. Remove the steak from the pan and leave to rest for 1-2 minutes. Sprinkle the lime juice over the vegetables and shake the pan to coat well.
6. Put everything on a plate, scatter over the coriander and serve with a lime wedge.

Beef curry

 4 serving  50 minutes

INGREDIENTS

- Low-calorie cooking spray
- 1 red onion, sliced
- 500g lean rump steak, cut into strips
- 1 red pepper, deseeded and chopped
- 1 tbsp madras curry powder*
- 2 level tbsp tomato purée
- 1 medium butternut squash, peeled and chopped
- 250g mushrooms, halved
- 275ml hot beef stock
- 200g dried basmati rice
- 150g fat-free natural yogurt
- Chopped fresh coriander, to serve

DIRECTIONS

1. Spray a non-stick saucepan with low-calorie cooking spray and place over a medium heat. Cook the onion for 10 minutes until softened. Add the steak strips and red peppers and cook, stirring, for 3 minutes. Add the curry powder and tomato purée and mix well.
2. Stir in the squash and the mushrooms, pour in the stock and bring to the boil. Cover and cook for 25 minutes.
3. Meanwhile, cook the rice according to the pack instructions.
4. Serve the curry drizzled with yogurt and scattered with coriander, along with the rice.

Beef hotpot bake

 4 serving 

3 hours 45 minutes

INGREDIENTS

- 750g lean stewing beef, visible fat removed, cubed
- 2 large onions, roughly chopped
- 2 carrots, roughly chopped
- 1 level tbsp plain flour
- 300ml hot beef stock
- 2 tsp Worcestershire sauce
- 400g can baked beans
- 2 bay leaves
- 600g potatoes, thickly sliced

DIRECTIONS

1. Preheat your oven to 180°C/fan 160°C/gas 4.
2. Place the beef, onions, carrots and flour in a baking dish, season lightly and toss to mix well.
3. Pour in the stock then add the Worcestershire sauce, baked beans and bay leaves. Stir to mix well and arrange the sliced potatoes on top of the meat mixture.
4. Cover with foil then place in the oven for 2½-3 hours or until the potatoes are cooked and tender.
5. Remove the foil, then turn the oven up to brown the potatoes for 20-30 minutes or brown under the grill for 5-8 minutes.

Beef stroganoff

 4 serving  45 minutes

INGREDIENTS

- 40g dried mushrooms
- Low-calorie cooking spray
- 2 onions, chopped
- 1 tbsp paprika
- 2 tsp smoked paprika
- 400g can cannellini beans, drained and rinsed
- 4 garlic cloves, chopped
- 150g cauliflower florets, chopped
- 500g fresh mushrooms, sliced
- 1 beef stock cube, crumbled
- 1 tbsp Bovril
- 1 tbsp Worcestershire sauce
- 1 tbsp white wine vinegar
- 100g plain quark
- 400g lean beef steak, visible fat removed, cut into thin strips
- 1 red onion, sliced
- 4 large gherkins, finely chopped
- Small pack fresh parsley, chopped

DIRECTIONS

1. Put the dried mushrooms in a heatproof jug and add 900ml boiling water. Set aside to soak for 20 minutes.
2. Meanwhile, place a large non-stick saucepan over a medium heat and spray with low-calorie cooking spray. Add the chopped onions and cook for a few minutes. Add the paprika, 1 tsp smoked paprika and a splash of water and cook for a further 2 minutes.
3. Add the beans, garlic, cauliflower and 200g of the fresh mushrooms, reduce the heat to low and cook for 2 minutes.
4. Add the stock cube and the dried mushrooms plus their soaking liquid and simmer for 15 minutes or until the beans and cauliflower are very soft.
5. Add the Bovril, Worcestershire sauce, vinegar and quark. Blitz until smooth using a stick blender (or use a food processor and return to the pan) and set aside.
6. Spray a large non-stick frying pan with low-calorie cooking spray and place over a high heat. Add the steak, red onion and the remaining smoked paprika and mushrooms. Cook for 5 minutes, then stir in your sauce and reduce the heat to a simmer.
7. Stir through the gherkins and parsley and serve hot with rice or your favourite vegetables.

Cottage pie

 4 serving  1 hour 10 minutes

INGREDIENTS

- Low-calorie cooking spray
- 500g lean beef mince (5% fat or less)
- 1 large onion, finely chopped
- 1 large carrot, finely chopped
- 2 celery sticks, finely chopped
- 2 large garlic cloves, crushed
- 1 beef stock cube, crumbled
- 3 tbsp tomato purée
- 2 tsp Worcestershire sauce
- ½ tsp dried thyme
- 1 tsp Marmite

For the topping:

- 800g potatoes, peeled and roughly chopped
- 200g parsnips, peeled and roughly chopped

DIRECTIONS

1. Spray a large non-stick frying pan with low-calorie cooking spray and place over a high heat. Add the beef and fry for 8-10 minutes or until nicely browned, breaking up any lumps. Drain off any fat, then transfer to a plate and keep warm.
2. Reduce the heat to medium and add the onion, carrot, celery, garlic and 2 tbsp water to the pan. Cook for 10 minutes, adding a little more water if anything starts to stick. Return the beef to the pan and add the stock cube, tomato purée, Worcestershire sauce, thyme, Marmite and 400ml boiling water. Bring to a simmer and cook for 20 minutes or until the sauce has thickened, stirring occasionally. Check the seasoning.
3. Meanwhile, make the topping. Put the potatoes and parsnips in a saucepan of cold water and bring to the boil over a high heat. Simmer for 15 minutes or until tender.
4. Once the potatoes and parsnips are cooking, preheat your oven to 200°C/fan 180°C/gas 6.
5. Spoon the beef mixture into an ovenproof dish. Drain the potatoes and parsnips, mash well and season to taste. Top the beef mixture with the mash and level the surface with a fork. Cook in the oven for 25 minutes. Divide between plates and serve with your favourite veg.

Chilli with rice

 4 serving  1 hour 45 minutes

INGREDIENTS

- Low-calorie cooking spray
- 2 onions, finely chopped
- 3 garlic cloves, finely chopped
- 800g lean beef mince (5% fat or less)
- 2 x 400g cans chopped tomatoes
- 4 tbsp tomato purée
- 2 tsp dried chilli flakes
- 1 tsp ground cumin
- 1 tsp ground coriander
- 1 cinnamon stick
- 1 tsp Worcestershire sauce
- 1 beef stock cube, crumbled
- 400g can red kidney beans in chilli sauce
- 400g can mixed beans, drained and rinsed
- 2 roasted red peppers in brine from a jar, drained and roughly chopped
- Large handful of fresh coriander, finely chopped, plus extra to serve
- 375g dried long-grain rice, cooked, to serve
- Fat-free natural yogurt, to serve
- Pinch of smoked paprika, to serve

DIRECTIONS

1. Spray a large, heavy-based non-stick pan with low-calorie cooking spray and place over a medium heat. Fry the onions and garlic for 4-5 minutes. Turn up the heat and brown the mince. Drain off any fat from the mince and return to the heat.
2. Stir in the tomatoes, tomato purée, chilli flakes, cumin, coriander, cinnamon stick, Worcestershire sauce and stock cube, and season lightly. Bring to a simmer, cover and reduce the heat to low. Cook for 45-50 minutes, stirring occasionally, until rich and thickened.
3. Stir in the kidney beans, mixed beans and pepper and cook, uncovered, for a further 10 minutes.
4. Divide the cooked rice and chilli between 4 wide bowls and garnish with coriander. Serve with the natural yogurt sprinkled with smoked paprika.

Cowboy hotpot

 4 serving  1 hour

INGREDIENTS

- 500g floury potatoes, such as King Edward or Maris Piper, thinly sliced
- Low-calorie cooking spray
- 12 Slimming World Pork Sausages, chopped into chunks
- 4 garlic cloves, chopped
- 1 large red onion, diced
- 2 red peppers, deseeded and diced
- 2 tbsp tomato purée
- 2 tbsp smoked paprika
- 1 chicken stock cube
- 400g can mixed beans in water
- 400g can baked beans
- 325g can sweetcorn kernels, drained
- 1 tbsp Marmite
- 1 tbsp Worcestershire sauce
- 1 tsp white wine vinegar
- Bunch spring onions, sliced

DIRECTIONS

1. Preheat your oven to 200°C/fan 180°C/gas 6.
2. Cook the potatoes in a saucepan of boiling water over a high heat for 5 minutes, then drain and set aside to cool.
3. Meanwhile, spray a large non-stick saucepan with low-calorie cooking spray and put it over a medium heat. Brown the sausages on all sides for 5 minutes, then add the garlic, onion and peppers and cook for 5 minutes, stirring occasionally. Stir in the tomato purée and smoked paprika and cook for 5 minutes.
4. Stir the stock cube into 200ml hot water, then add to the sausage pan along with the mixed beans, baked beans, sweetcorn, Marmite, Worcestershire sauce, vinegar and spring onions. Simmer for 5 minutes, then transfer to an ovenproof dish and top with the potatoes. Spray with low-calorie cooking spray and cook in the oven for 30 minutes. Serve hot, with your favourite Speed vegetables.

Scotch eggs

 4 serving  50 minutes

INGREDIENTS

- 2 packs Slimming World Pork Sausages
- 1-2 tsp curry powder*
- 2 tbsp dried parsley
- 1 tsp mixed herbs
- 4 hard-boiled eggs
- 2 eggs, beaten
- 50g wholemeal bread, whizzed into fine crumbs
- Low-calorie cooking spray

*Watch out for spice/seasoning blends that have added ingredients (like sugar, oil or starch). To protect your weight loss, count ½ Syn per level tsp/1½ Syns per level tbsp.

DIRECTIONS

1. Skin the sausages (it's less messy if the meat is still frozen). Mix together the sausage meat, curry powder and dried herbs either in a bowl or in the food processor and season lightly. Divide the mixture into 4 portions.
2. Preheat your oven to 200°C/fan 180°C/gas 6.
3. Flatten a portion of the mixture in your right hand and, with your left hand, take an egg and wrap the mince around it until it's fully encased. Repeat for the remaining 3 boiled eggs.
4. Beat the remaining eggs and dip each Scotch egg in the beaten egg, then roll in the breadcrumbs. Place on a baking sheet lined with baking parchment and lightly spray with low-calorie cooking spray.
5. Place the Scotch eggs in the oven and cook for 20 minutes or until lightly golden. Eat hot, or cool completely on kitchen paper and then cover and chill until you're ready to eat.

Toad-in-the-hole

 4 serving  1 hour

INGREDIENTS

- 12 Slimming World Pork Sausages
- Low-calorie cooking spray
- 1 large onion, sliced into rings
- 60g plain flour
- 2 level tsp baking powder
- 100ml skimmed milk
- 5 large eggs
- 2 fresh rosemary sprigs, leaves roughly chopped
- 2 tsp dried sage
- 1kg floury potatoes, such as Maris Piper or King Edward, cut into large chunks
- 1 chicken or vegetable stock cube, crumbled
- Slimming World Roasted Onion Gravy (available from Iceland), to serve
- 300g green beans, trimmed

DIRECTIONS

1. Preheat your oven to 220°C/fan 200°C/gas 7. Spread the sausages out in a large, non-stick roasting tin in a single layer. Spray with low-calorie cooking spray and cook for 10 minutes.
2. Turn over the sausages, then scatter the onion rings over the top. Spray lightly with a little more low-calorie cooking spray and return to the oven for a further 15 minutes.
3. Meanwhile, sieve the flour and baking powder into a mixing bowl or a large jug. Use a hand whisk to mix in the milk very gradually, followed by 75ml water to make a smooth, lump-free batter.
4. Whisk in the eggs, one at a time, until the batter is well combined (it should be a smooth, pourable consistency). Stir in the rosemary and sage, and season lightly.
5. When the sausages are cooked, remove the tin from the oven and quickly pour the batter around them. Return the tin to the oven. Reduce the oven temperature to 200°C/fan 180°C/gas 6 and bake for 25 minutes, or until the batter is puffed up and golden.
6. Meanwhile, cook the potatoes with the stock cube in a pan of boiling water for 10-12 minutes. Reserve 100ml stock water, then drain. Return the potatoes to the pan, season lightly and mash with the reserved stock. Heat the gravy according to the pack instructions. Boil the beans for 5-6 minutes, then drain. To serve, divide everything between 4 plates.

BBQ pulled pork

 4 serving  8 hours 25 minutes

INGREDIENTS

- 500g passata
- 5 tbsp Worcestershire sauce
- 3 tbsp balsamic vinegar
- 1 tsp mustard powder
- 2 garlic cloves, crushed
- 3 level tbsp sweetener
- 1.5-2kg pork shoulder, visible fat removed

DIRECTIONS

1. In a small bowl, mix the passata, Worcestershire sauce, balsamic vinegar, mustard powder, garlic, sweetener and seasoning. Transfer to a small pan and simmer for 15 minutes, or until the sauce thickens.
2. Meanwhile, heat a non-stick frying pan until hot, then sear the pork on all sides. Transfer to a slow cooker, coat with the sauce and cook for 8-12 hours on low.
3. Remove the pork from the slow cooker and place on a cutting board. Allow the meat to cool for approximately 15 minutes, then shred into bite-sized pieces using two forks.
4. Remove the sauce from the pan and set aside to drizzle over the meat later.

Lancashire hotpot

 4 serving  2 hours 30 minutes

INGREDIENTS

- Low-calorie cooking spray
- 8 lean lamb leg steaks, visible fat removed, cut into bite-size pieces
- 3 large onions, roughly chopped
- 4 celery sticks, roughly chopped
- 4 large carrots, roughly chopped
- 1 level tbsp plain flour
- 1 tbsp Worcestershire sauce
- 4 tbsp tomato purée
- 500ml hot lamb stock
- 2 bay leaves
- 800g potatoes, thinly sliced
- Handful fresh parsley, finely chopped, to serve

DIRECTIONS

1. Preheat your oven to 160°C/fan 140°C/gas 3.
2. Put a large non-stick casserole dish sprayed with low-calorie cooking spray over a high heat. Cook the lamb in 2 batches for 3-4 minutes each, or until browned. Transfer to a plate with a slotted spoon, cover and set aside.
3. Add the onions, celery and carrots to the dish and stir-fry for 3-4 minutes. Sprinkle over the flour and cook for a further 2 minutes. Add the Worcestershire sauce, tomato purée and stock, and bring to the boil.
4. Return the lamb to the dish, stir in the bay leaves and remove from the heat. Arrange the sliced potatoes on top of the meat and veg, cover and cook in the oven for 1½ hours, or until the potatoes and lamb are tender.
5. Turn up the heat to 200°C/fan 180°C/gas 6, spray the potatoes with low-calorie cooking spray and cook the hotpot for a further 10 minutes, uncovered, until golden. Garnish with the parsley and serve.

Rice, Pasta & Noodles

Singapore style noodle 89

Smoky meatball tagliatelle 90

Macaroni cheese 91

Spaghetti bolognese 92

Ratatouille pasta bake 93

Healthy tuna pasta 94

Vegetable stir-fry noodles 95

Carbonara 96

Pork & noodle stir-fry 97

Pasta lentilognese 98

Salt & pepper hicken chow mein 99

Prawn stir-fry 100

Cupboard love tuna pasta 101

Chicken chow mein 102

Egg fried rice 103

Tuna pasta bake 104

Teriyaki chicken & rice bowl 105

Singapore-style noodles

 4 serving  30 minutes

INGREDIENTS

- 2 onions, 1 roughly chopped, 1 finely sliced
- 4 garlic cloves
- 1 red chilli, deseeded
- 2.5cm piece fresh root ginger, peeled and roughly chopped
- 4 tbsp medium curry powder*
- 1 tbsp ground turmeric
- 1 tbsp Chinese five-spice powder*
- 1 tbsp Thai fish sauce (nam pla)
- 200g lean pork loin, visible fat removed, cut into thin strips
- 2 skinless and boneless chicken breasts, cut into thin strips
- 250g dried noodles
- 2 carrots, cut into batons
- 2 red peppers, deseeded and sliced
- 150g sugar snap peas
- 3 tbsp soy sauce
- 2 tbsp rice wine vinegar

DIRECTIONS

1. Put the chopped onion in your food processor and add the garlic, chilli, ginger, curry powder, turmeric, five-spice and fish sauce and blitz into a fine paste (you can also do this in a bowl using a stick blender).
2. Put the pork and chicken in a bowl and add one-third of your spice paste. Stir to coat well and leave to marinate for at least 5 minutes.
3. At the same time, cook the noodles according to the pack instructions then drain well, rinse under cold running water and drain again.
4. Spray a non-stick frying pan or wok with low-calorie cooking spray and put it over a high heat. Add the chicken and pork and cook for about 5 minutes, adding a splash of water if anything starts to stick. Transfer to a plate and set aside.
5. Reduce the heat to medium and spray the frying pan or wok with a little more low-calorie cooking spray. Add the rest of your spice paste and cook for 2 minutes, then add the carrots, peppers, sugar snaps, sliced onion and 400ml boiling water. Cook for a few minutes or until softened.
6. Return the pork and chicken to the pan, add the cooked noodles and stir together until everything is hot. Add the soy sauce and vinegar to serve.

Smoky meatball tagliatelle

 4 serving  45 minutes

INGREDIENTS

- Low-calorie cooking spray
- 320g bag frozen Slimming World Italian-style Beef & Pork Meatballs
- 1 large onion, finely chopped
- 4 celery sticks, finely chopped
- 2 garlic cloves, finely chopped
- 1 tsp hot smoked paprika
- 1 tbsp tomato purée
- 2 x 400g cans chopped tomatoes
- 300g dried tagliatelle
- ½ pack fresh basil, shredded, reserving a few small whole leaves to serve

DIRECTIONS

1. Spray a large, lidded flameproof casserole dish with low-calorie cooking spray and place over a medium heat. Cook the meatballs for 5-8 minutes until browned all over, then remove and set aside.
2. Spray the dish with a little more low-calorie cooking spray and add the onion and celery. Cook for 2 minutes then cover and cook for a further 8-10 minutes, stirring occasionally, until the vegetables are soft. Stir in the garlic, paprika and tomato purée and cook for an extra minute until fragrant.
3. Add the chopped tomatoes and meatballs and bring to the boil. Cover, reduce to a simmer and cook for 10 minutes. Meanwhile, cook the pasta according to the packet instructions, then drain.
4. Stir the shredded basil into the sauce then divide the pasta between 4 bowls. Scatter over the reserved basil leaves and freshly ground black pepper to serve.

Macaroni cheese

 4 serving  1 hour

INGREDIENTS

- 300g dried macaroni
- Low-calorie cooking spray
- 1 red onion, finely chopped
- 2 garlic cloves, finely chopped
- 1 roasted red pepper in brine from a jar, finely chopped
- 1 courgette, coarsely grated
- 400ml vegetable stock
- 4 tbsp tomato purée
- 200g fat-free natural cottage cheese
- 1 tsp English mustard powder mixed with 1 tsp water
- 2 eggs, lightly beaten
- 160g reduced-fat Cheddar, coarsely grated
- A salad of mixed leaves and thinly sliced yellow peppers, to serve

DIRECTIONS

1. Preheat your oven to 200°C/fan 180°C/gas 6.
2. Cook the macaroni according to the pack instructions, then drain well and tip into a wide mixing bowl.
3. Meanwhile, place a large non-stick frying pan sprayed with low-cooking spray over a high heat. Add the onion, garlic, red pepper and courgette, and cook, stirring for 2-3 minutes. Add to the macaroni.
4. Put the stock, tomato purée, cottage cheese, mustard and eggs in a jug and whisk until smooth. Pour this over the macaroni mixture, then stir in three-quarters of the Cheddar. Season and toss well.
5. Transfer to a shallow, ovenproof dish. Sprinkle over the remaining Cheddar and bake for 15-20 minutes, or until bubbling and golden. Allow to rest for 5 minutes, then serve with the salad.

Spaghetti bolognese

 4 serving  55 minutes

INGREDIENTS

- 2 lean back bacon rashers, visible fat removed, roughly chopped
- 2 onions, roughly chopped
- 2 carrots, peeled and diced
- 2 celery sticks, roughly chopped
- 2 garlic cloves, crushed
- 500g lean beef mince (5% fat or less)
- 2 x 400g cans chopped tomatoes
- 2 tsp dried oregano
- 1 beef stock cube
- 500g dried spaghetti
- 4 level tbsp grated fresh Parmesan, to serve
- Fresh basil leaves, to serve
- Mixed salad, to serve

DIRECTIONS

1. Put a large non-stick frying pan over a medium-high heat. Add the bacon, onions, carrots, celery, garlic and 2 tbsp water and stir-fry for about 7 minutes, adding a splash more water if needed.
2. Add the beef, breaking it up with a spoon, and cook for 3 minutes or until browned. Drain off any fat in the pan, then add the chopped tomatoes and oregano, crumble in the stock cube and bring to the boil. Cover, reduce the heat to low and simmer for 30 minutes.
3. When the sauce has about 10 minutes to go, cook the spaghetti according to the pack instructions.
4. Drain the spaghetti and divide between shallow bowls. Season the sauce to taste and spoon it over the spaghetti. Evenly scatter over the Parmesan and basil and serve hot with the salad.

Ratatouille pasta bake

 4 serving  1 hour 15 minutes

INGREDIENTS

- low-calorie cooking spray
- 2 red peppers, deseeded and chopped into chunks
- 2 red onions, cut into wedges
- 2 aubergines, chopped into chunks
- 2 courgettes, chopped into chunks
- 2 x 400g cans chopped tomatoes
- 2 garlic cloves, crushed
- 300g dried pasta shapes (we used fusilli)
- 280g reduced-fat mozzarella, torn into small pieces
- ½ small pack fresh basil, to serve

DIRECTIONS

1. Preheat your oven to 200°C/fan 180°C/gas 6 and spray a large, non-stick baking tray with low-calorie cooking spray. Add the peppers, onions, aubergines and courgettes and spread them out. Spray the veg with low-calorie cooking spray and roast for 40 minutes, until caramelised and soft, turning halfway.
2. While they're roasting, put the tomatoes in a large non-stick saucepan along with the garlic. Bring to a simmer and cook for 10 minutes, until reduced and thickened. Season lightly and set aside. Now boil the pasta for 3 minutes less than the pack instructions (it will finish cooking in the oven), then drain and toss into the tomato sauce.
3. Once the vegetables are ready, stir them through the pasta mixture, then spoon everything into a large baking dish. Evenly scatter over the mozzarella and bake for 20-25 minutes or until the mozzarella has melted and is turning golden. Season with freshly ground black pepper and scatter over the basil leaves. Divide between 4 plates and serve with the rocket.

Healthy tuna pasta

2 servings 24 minutes

INGREDIENTS

- 150g wholemeal penne
- 1 large leek (200g), halved, and thinly sliced
- 1 tsp olive oil
- 160g cherry tomatoes, preferably on the vine
- 198g can sweetcorn, drained
- 75g ricotta
- 160g can tuna in spring water, drained
- handful of basil, chopped, plus a few whole leaves to serve

DIRECTIONS

1. Boil the penne with the leek in a large pan of salted water following pack instructions, until al dente.
2. Meanwhile, heat the oil in a large pan over a medium-high heat and fry the tomatoes for a few minutes, until they start to burst and soften. Add the sweetcorn and cook for 2-3 mins to heat through. Drain the pasta and leeks, reserving a little of the pasta water. Tip the drained pasta and leeks into the pan with the tomatoes, then toss through the ricotta and tuna.
3. Season with plenty of black pepper. If you want to loosen the consistency, stir in some of the reserved pasta water along with the chopped basil. Serve scattered with the whole basil leaves.

Vegetable Stir Fry Noodles

 4 servings  25 minutes

INGREDIENTS

- 225g Medium Egg Noodles [Uncooked Weight]
- Frylight/Low Calorie Cooking Spray
- ¼ tsp Ground Dried Ginger
- 3 Garlic Cloves
- 150g Button Mushrooms
- 1 Carrot
- 1 Red Pepper
- 1 [Approx 373g] Head of broccoli
- ½ tsp Onion Powder
- ½ tsp Smoked Paprika
- ½ tsp Hot Chilli Powder
- 150ml Boiling vegetable stock
- 4 tbsp Dark Soy Sauce [Light would work okay too]
- 2 tbsp Rice Vinegar
- 2 tbsp Oyster Sauce
- Pinch Salt
- 1 tbsp Granulated Sweetener

DIRECTIONS

1. Cook noodles as per instruction, al dente, do not overcook.
2. Meanwhile spritz a pan with Frylight and sauté ginger and garlic over a medium heat for 2 minutes.
3. Add onion powder, smoked paprika, chilli powder and all vegetables to the pan. Continue to sauté for 5 minutes. If the vegetables start to burn add a splash of water or vegetable stock .
4. In a bowl add stock, soy sauce. rice vinegar, oyster sauce, salt and sweetener. Whisk together and then add to the pan. Allow to simmer over a medium heat for 2 – 3 minutes stirring often.
5. Throw in the cooked noodles and toss the ingredients together. Cook for 1 – 2 minutes and then serve.

Carbonara

 4 serving  20 minutes

INGREDIENTS

- 400g dried spaghetti
- 6 back bacon rashers, visible fat removed
- 4 eggs*
- 4 tbsp fat-free natural fromage frais
- 2 level tbsp grated fresh Parmesan
- Small handful of fresh chives, finely snipped

DIRECTIONS

1. Cook the spaghetti according to the pack instructions. Drain well and return to the saucepan.
2. Meanwhile, place a large non-stick frying pan over a high heat. Add the bacon and dry-fry for 2-3 minutes, then turn off the heat.
3. Lightly beat the eggs, season lightly and stir in the fromage frais, 1 level tbsp Parmesan and most of the chives.
4. Add the bacon to the drained spaghetti and mix well over a low heat, then remove from the heat and stir in the egg mixture. Toss thoroughly so that the eggs thicken in the residual heat, making a sauce that coats the pasta.
5. Divide the spaghetti between 4 bowls, then divide over the remaining Parmesan and chives. Serve hot.

Pork and noodle stir-fry

 4 serving  35 minutes

INGREDIENTS

- 250g dried medium egg noodles
- 500g lean pork mince (5% fat or less)
- 2 garlic cloves, finely grated
- 2 tsp finely grated fresh root ginger
- 1 red chilli, deseeded and thinly sliced
- 1 tbsp dark soy sauce
- 2 tbsp light soy sauce
- 1 level tbsp sweet chilli sauce
- Low-calorie cooking spray
- 2 x 225g cans sliced water chestnuts in water, drained
- 300g pack stir-fry vegetables
- Lime wedges, to serve

DIRECTIONS

1. Cook the noodles according to the pack instructions. Drain well, cover and set aside.
2. Mix together the pork, garlic and ginger. Add the chilli, both soy sauces and the sweet chilli sauce and mix well again.
3. Spray a large non-stick frying pan or wok with low-calorie cooking spray and place over a high heat. Add the pork mixture and stir-fry for 2-3 minutes.
4. Add the water chestnuts and stir-fry veg. Stir-fry for 4-5 minutes, or until the vegetables are just tender and the pork is cooked through. Stir in the noodles to warm through, then remove from the heat. Divide between 4 bowls and serve with the lime wedges for squeezing over.

Pasta lentilognese

 4 serving 

INGREDIENTS

- Low-calorie cooking spray
- 1 medium carrot, diced
- 1 celery stick, diced
- 2 medium red onions, 1 diced and 1 cut into wedges
- 2 tsp dried oregano
- 4 garlic cloves, chopped
- 2 tbsp tomato purée
- 1 vegetable stock cube, suitable for vegans
- 400g can chopped tomatoes
- 1 tbsp yeast extract
- 1 medium courgette, diced
- 300g mushrooms, sliced
- 300g dried linguine or spaghetti
- 2 x 400g cans green lentils, drained and rinsed
- 500g cherry tomatoes
- ½ large bag rocket leaves

DIRECTIONS

1. Spray a medium non-stick saucepan with low-calorie cooking spray and put it over a medium heat. Add the carrot, celery and diced onion and cook for 2 minutes. Stir in the oregano, garlic, tomato purée and some freshly ground black pepper, reduce the heat to low and simmer for 5 minutes.
2. Dissolve the stock cube in 3 tbsp boiling water and add to the pan, along with the chopped tomatoes and the yeast extract. Cover and cook for 10 minutes.
3. Add the onion wedges, courgette and mushrooms and cover again. Bring back to a simmer and cook for 10 minutes.
4. Meanwhile, cook the pasta according to the pack instructions.
5. Stir the lentils and cherry tomatoes into the vegetables, simmer for 5 minutes and season to taste. Drain the pasta and stir through the vegetables along with the rocket. Cook it all for 2 minutes then serve hot, with a Speed salad.

Salt and pepper chicken chow mein

 4 serving  45 minutes

INGREDIENTS

- Low-calorie cooking spray
- 2 medium onions, diced
- 4 garlic cloves, roughly chopped
- 5cm piece fresh root ginger, peeled and roughly chopped
- 1 heaped tbsp Chinese five-spice powder*
- 2 tbsp tomato purée
- 1 carrot, cut into batons
- 4 tbsp dark soy sauce
- 1 tbsp Marmite
- 2 peppers (red and yellow), deseeded and sliced
- 4 skinless and boneless chicken breasts, thinly sliced
- 4 dried noodle nests
- 300g fresh bean sprouts, rinsed
- Bunch spring onions, chopped
- Small pack fresh coriander, chopped, reserving a few sprigs to serve

DIRECTIONS

1. Spray a non-stick wok or saucepan with low-calorie cooking spray and put it over a medium heat. Add the onions and cook for 5 minutes.
2. Meanwhile, put the garlic, ginger and 100ml water in your food processor and blitz to a smooth paste.
3. Add the garlic-ginger paste to the onions along with the five-spice powder and 1 tsp freshly ground black pepper and cook for 5 minutes. Stir in the tomato purée and 200ml hot water, then add the carrots and bring back to a simmer. Cover and cook for 5 minutes.
4. Stir in the soy sauce, Marmite and peppers and cook for 5 minutes. Add the chicken, cover again and cook for 10 minutes or until the chicken is cooked through, stirring occasionally.
5. While the chicken is cooking, prepare the noodles according to the pack instructions and drain well.
6. Add the noodles, bean sprouts, spring onions and coriander to the chicken and cook for 3 minutes, then serve hot with the coriander sprigs for scattering over and with your favourite Speed veg.

Prawn stir fry

 4 serving 

20 minutes

INGREDIENTS

- 2 level tsp cornflour
- 1 tsp chopped garlic in vinegar from a jar, drained
- 1 tbsp chopped ginger in vinegar from a jar, drained
- 1 level tbsp hot chilli sauce, such as sriracha
- 2 tbsp dark soy sauce
- 1 tbsp oyster sauce
- Pinch of sweetener granules
- 1 tbsp tomato purée
- 100ml boiling chicken stock
- Low-calorie cooking spray
- 200g frozen sliced red onions
- 300g frozen mixed sliced peppers
- 200g frozen green beans
- 250g dried egg noodles
- 400g frozen cooked and peeled prawns, thawed
- 225g can sliced bamboo shoots, drained

DIRECTIONS

1. Mix together the cornflour, garlic, ginger, chilli sauce, soy sauce, oyster sauce, sweetener, tomato purée and stock in a small bowl.
2. Spray a deep non-stick frying pan or wok with low-calorie cooking spray and place over a high heat. When hot, add the onions, peppers and 2 tbsp water and stir-fry for 4 minutes. Add the green beans and stir-fry for 3 minutes, or until all the vegetables are just tender.
3. Meanwhile, cook the noodles according to the pack instructions and drain well.
4. Add the prawns and bamboo shoots to the vegetables and stir-fry for 1-2 minutes, then add the noodles and the chilli sauce mixture and toss well. Simmer for 1 minute, or until the sauce has thickened.
5. Divide between 4 bowls and serve piping hot.

Cupboard love tuna pasta

4 servings 20 minutes

INGREDIENTS

- 400g dried pasta shapes
- Low-calorie cooking spray
- 4 spring onions, thinly sliced
- 1 red chilli, deseeded and finely chopped
- 2 garlic cloves, finely chopped
- 4 tomatoes, roughly chopped (or use a 400g can chopped tomatoes)
- 340g can sweetcorn kernels, drained
- 400g can tuna in spring water or brine, drained and flaked
- Chopped fresh dill, to serve (optional)

DIRECTIONS

1. Cook the pasta according to the pack instructions and drain well, reserving 1-2 tbsp of the cooking water.
2. Once the pasta is going, spray a deep non-stick frying pan with low-calorie cooking spray and put it over a medium heat. Add the spring onions, chilli and garlic and stir-fry for 1-2 minutes, then add the tomatoes and sweetcorn and cook for 2-3 minutes. Stir in the tuna and cook for another 2-3 minutes.
3. Add the pasta and reserved cooking water to the tuna and toss it all together. Season to taste, scatter over the dill, if using, and serve with salad.

Chicken Chow Mein

 4 servings  45 minutes

INGREDIENTS

- 4 tbsp light soy sauce
- 1 level tbsp hot chilli sauce
- 2 tsp Chinese rice vinegar or white wine vinegar
- 4 garlic cloves, crushed
- 2cm piece root ginger, peeled and finely grated
- 1 level tsp Chinese five-spice powder* (see tip)
- 3 large skinless and boneless chicken breasts, thinly sliced
- 200g dried medium or thin egg noodles
- Low-calorie cooking spray
- 200g mangetout, halved lengthways
- 225g can water chestnuts, drained
- 225g can bamboo shoots, drained
- 1 red pepper, deseeded and thinly sliced
- 8 spring onions, sliced diagonally
- 1 level tbsp sweet chilli sauce
- 4 tbsp dark soy sauce
- Thinly sliced red chillies, to serve (optional)

DIRECTIONS

1. Place the light soy sauce in a large bowl and stir in the hot chilli sauce, vinegar, garlic, ginger and five-spice powder. Add the chicken and stir to coat in the dressing. Leave to marinate for 10 minutes.
2. Meanwhile, cook the noodles according to the pack instructions and drain well.
3. Spray a large non-stick wok or frying pan with low-calorie cooking spray, add the chicken mixture and stir-fry over a high heat for 4-5 minutes, or until lightly browned.
4. Add all the vegetables and stir-fry for a further 4-5 minutes.
5. Add the noodles, sweet chilli sauce and dark soy sauce and cook for a further 4 minutes, or until piping hot. Divide between 4 bowls and serve immediately with sliced red chillies on the side, if using.

Egg Fried Rice

 4 servings  20 minutes

INGREDIENTS

- Low-calorie cooking spray
- 350g dried long-grain or jasmine rice, cooked and cooled
- 200g frozen peas
- 2 eggs, lightly beaten
- 3 tbsp light soy sauce/tamari
- 400g fresh bean sprouts, washed
- 6 spring onions, very finely sliced

DIRECTIONS

1. Spray a non-stick wok or large frying pan with low-calorie cooking spray and put it over a high heat. When it's almost at smoking point, add the cooked rice and stir-fry for about 3 minutes.
2. Add the peas, stir-fry for 5 minutes and season lightly. Add the beaten eggs and stir-fry for another minute.
3. Stir in the soy sauce, bean sprouts and most of the spring onions and cook for 2 minutes or until the eggs have set.
4. Scatter over the remaining spring onions to serve.

Tuna pasta bake

 4 servings 35 minutes

INGREDIENTS

- 350g dried fusilli pasta
- 1 small leek, thinly sliced
- 100g frozen spinach
- 100g frozen sweetcorn
- 250g plain quark
- 175g fat-free natural fromage frais
- 400g canned tuna chunks in spring water, drained
- 75g reduced-fat Cheddar, grated

DIRECTIONS

1. Preheat your grill to its highest setting. Cook the pasta in a large pan of lightly salted boiling water for 8 minutes. After 4 minutes, add the leek, spinach and sweetcorn, making sure the water comes back to the boil quickly. Drain the pasta and vegetables and tip back into the pan.
2. Stir the quark, fromage frais and tuna chunks into the pasta with half of the cheese and some seasoning.
3. Spoon the pasta into a large ovenproof dish, sprinkle over the remaining cheese and place on a baking tray. Grill for 10 minutes until the cheese is melted and browning.
4. Serve with salad or fresh veggies.

Teriyaki Chicken and Rice Bowl

 2 servings  30 minutes

INGREDIENTS

- ½ red pepper, diced
- ½ green pepper diced
- 1 small carrot, diced
- ½ courgette, diced
- 180g (6oz) of uncooked boneless skinless chicken thigh
- 1.5 tablespoon of light soy sauce
- 2 teaspoons of dark soy sauce
- 2 tablespoons of maple syrup
- 1 tablespoon of rice vinegar
- 1 teaspoon ground ginger
- ½ teaspoon of garlic powder
- ½ teaspoon of onion powder
- ¼ cup (60ml) of water
- 2 spring onions roughly chopped
- 250g (9oz) of cooked and chilled long grain rice (day old is best)
- 1 teaspoon of sesame oil
- cooking oil spray

DIRECTIONS

1. Slice the chicken thighs into small bite size pieces.
2. Place in a bowl and cover with the ginger, garlic powder and onion powder, soy sauce, water, rice vinegar, and maple syrup and stir to coat.
3. Spray a frying pan over a medium high heat with some cooking oil spray
4. Add the chicken with the marinade and simmer until sauce reduces and thickens and chicken is cooked through, remove from pan and set aside
5. Wipe pan clean.
6. Spray with more cooking oil spray.
7. Add all the vegetables and stir fry for 2 mins.
8. Add the rice and mix to combine.
9. Make a space in the centre and add the chicken with the sauce back to the pan and start stirring to evenly mix everything together. Add in the sesame oil and toss to coat.
10. Serve in bowls and top with chopped spring onion.

Seafood

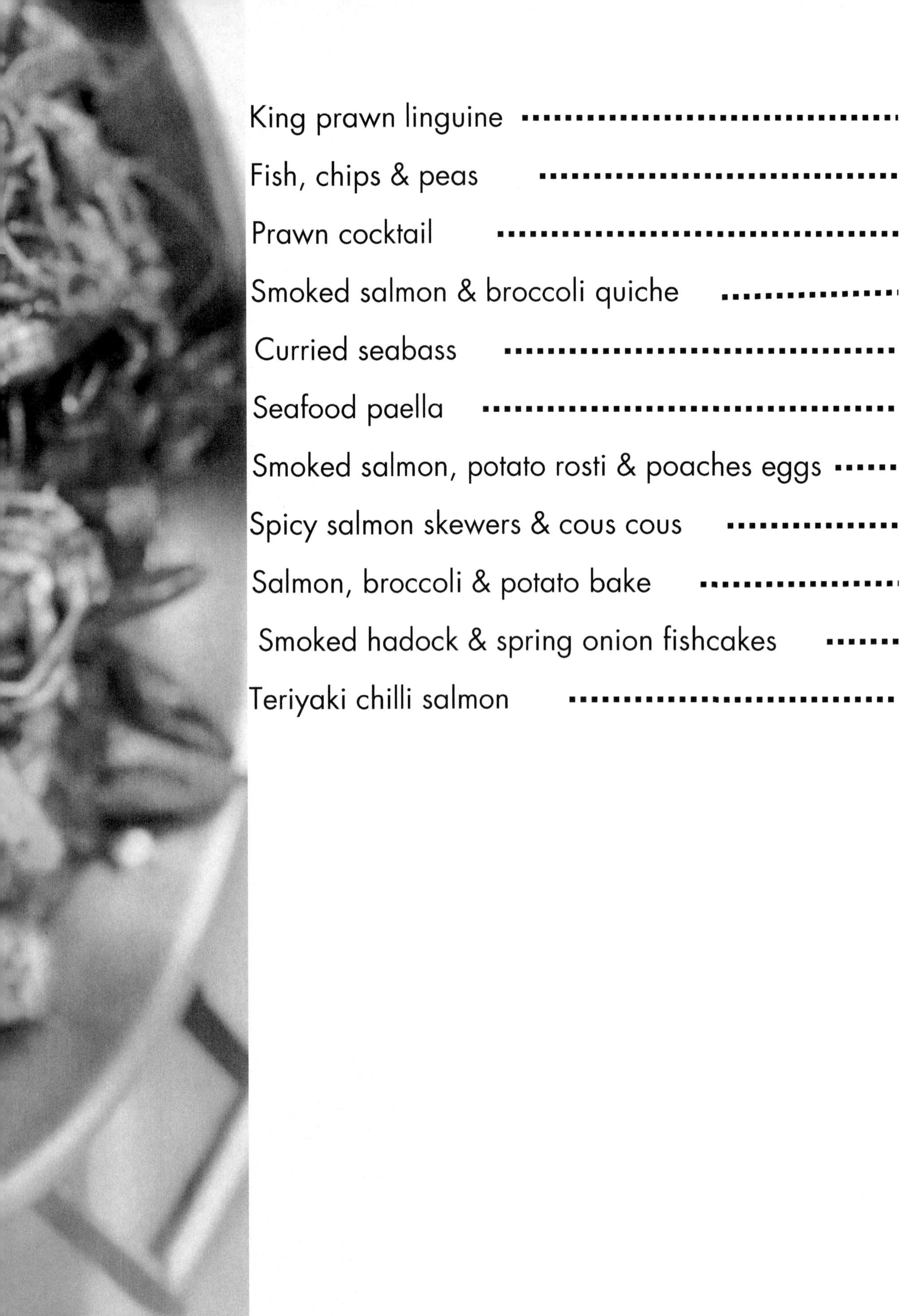

King prawn linguine 108

Fish, chips & peas 109

Prawn cocktail 110

Smoked salmon & broccoli quiche 111

Curried seabass 112

Seafood paella 113

Smoked salmon, potato rosti & poaches eggs 114

Spicy salmon skewers & cous cous 115

Salmon, broccoli & potato bake 116

Smoked hadock & spring onion fishcakes 117

Teriyaki chilli salmon 118

King prawn linguine

 4 serving  45 minutes

INGREDIENTS

- Low-calorie cooking spray
- 2 large red peppers, deseeded and roughly chopped
- 1 large yellow pepper, deseeded and roughly chopped
- 1 large onion, roughly chopped
- 3 garlic cloves, crushed
- ¼ tsp dried chilli flakes
- 1 tsp dried oregano
- ½ tsp smoked paprika
- 3 tbsp tomato purée
- 400g can chopped tomatoes
- 1 vegetable stock cube
- 1 tsp balsamic vinegar
- 400g dried linguine pasta
- 200g cherry tomatoes, halved
- 400g peeled raw king prawns

DIRECTIONS

1. Spray a large non-stick saucepan with low-calorie cooking spray and place over a medium heat. Add the peppers and onion and cook for 10 minutes, stirring occasionally and adding a splash of water if anything starts to stick.
2. Stir in all the remaining ingredients except the linguine, cherry tomatoes and prawns. Add 350ml boiling water, reduce the heat to low and simmer for 15 minutes, stirring occasionally.
3. Meanwhile, cook the pasta according to the pack instructions and drain.
4. Add the cherry tomatoes and prawns to the sauce and simmer for a further 5-8 minutes or until the prawns are pink and cooked through. Season lightly and serve hot with a salad.

Fish, chips & peas

 4 serving 

INGREDIENTS

- 3 medium slices day-old white bread from a small 400g loaf, torn into pieces
- 800g floury potatoes, such as Desiree or King Edward, cut into thick chips
- Low-calorie cooking spray
- 4 x skinless and boneless cod fillets
- 2 eggs
- 2 level tbsp beer
- Small handful fresh parsley, finely chopped, to serve
- Mushy peas, canned, to serve
- Lemon wedges, to serve

DIRECTIONS

1. Preheat your oven to 220°C/fan 200°C/gas 7. Line 2 baking trays with baking paper. Whizz the bread in a food processor until crumbed, then tip onto a plate.
2. Cook the chips in boiling water for 4-5 minutes, then drain well, return to the pan and cover. Lightly shake to roughen up the edges, then arrange on 1 of the baking trays in a single layer. Spray with low-calorie cooking spray, season and bake for 15-20 minutes, or until golden.
3. While they're cooking, season the cod. In a shallow bowl, beat together the eggs and beer. Dip the fish in the egg mixture, then coat with the breadcrumbs. Transfer to the second baking sheet. Repeat with the remaining fillets and bake for 15-20 minutes, or until cooked through and lightly browned
4. Sprinkle the parsley over the fish and serve with the chips, plenty of mushy peas, plus lemon wedges for squeezing over.

Prawn Cocktail

 2 servings  10 minutes

INGREDIENTS

- 170 g large cooked peeled prawns
- 3 tbsp Arla Cherry Tomato & Basil Quark Cooking Cheese or add a little tomato puree and some dried basil to plain quark
- ½ tbsp white wine vinegar
- ½ tbsp tomato puree
- ½ lemon cut into 3 wedges
- 1 dash Worcestershire sauce
- freshly ground black pepper to taste
- 1 pinch paprika or cayenne Pepper
- 1 pickled gherkin finely chopped
- 4 leaves little gem lettuce or you could use Iceberg if you prefer
- fresh parsley for garnish
- 2 slices cucumber
- 1 cherry tomato cut in half

DIRECTIONS

1. Mix all the ingredients (except the prawns, lettuce, lemon and parsley) together in a bowl. Squeeze in the juice from one of the lemon wedges. Check the seasoning and add a little more black pepper if needed
2. Arrange the salad leaves on a plate or in a bowl
3. Stir the prawns into the sauce, then arrange them neatly on each leaf. Spoon over the remaining sauce, then garnish with the cucumber, tomato and lemon wedges and serve

Smoked Salmon and Broccoli Quiche

 6 servings  25 minutes

INGREDIENTS

- 8 large eggs
- 1 medium head of broccoli
- 4-6 slices smoked salmon chopped into small pieces
- 2 spring onions
- 2 tbsp quark
- 1 pinch salt
- 1 pinch black pepper
- low calorie cooking spray

DIRECTIONS

1. Preheat oven to 190°C. Cut the broccoli into small florets and cook for 3-4 minutes, in the steamer or in the pan.
2. Drain and pat dry with a kitchen roll. Allow to cool.
3. Chop the spring onions and fry off in a bit of low calorie cooking spray until they soften.
4. In a bowl mix the eggs, quark, salt and pepper until it's smooth and no lumps.
5. In a silicone mould, place the broccoli, smoked salmon and spring onion. Then pour over the egg mix.
6. Bake for 20-25 minutes at 190°C or until set and golden on the top.

Curried Seabass

 2 servings  10 minutes

INGREDIENTS

- 2 seabass fillets
- 1 tsp cumin seeds
- 1 tbsp garam masala
- low calorie cooking spray

DIRECTIONS

1. On the skin side of the seabass fillets, spray with low calorie cooking spray and sprinkle over the cumin seeds and garam masala.
2. Mist a frying pan with low calorie cooking spray and place the seabass fillets skin side down into the frying pan. Cook on this side for 4 minutes on a moderate heat - don't be tempted to move them or turn them sooner or the skin won't be crisp. Flip the fish over after 4 minutes and cook for 1 minute on the flesh side.
3. Serve immediately with rice, salad and a wedge of lime.

Seafood Paella

 3 servings  30minutes

INGREDIENTS

- 300 grams paella rice you can use risotto rice if you can't get paella rice
- 1 red onion finely chopped
- 1 red pepper cut into strips
- 100 grams green beans cut in half
- 100 grams peas
- 1 clove garlic finely crushed
- 100 grams king prawns
- 1 packet Lidl Ocean Sea Scottish Cooked Mussels in a White Wine Sauce
- 6 Lidl Fantail Prawns
- 1 Lidl Chicken Breast cut into pieces
- 600 ml chicken stock made up with 2 Chicken Oxo Cubes
- 1 tsp paprika
- 1 lemon Cut into 6 wedges
- low calorie cooking spray
- sea salt to taste

DIRECTIONS

1. In a paella pan or very large frying pan, spray a little low calorie and cook the chicken until it starts to brown.
2. Add the onion and garlic to the pan and continue to cook until it's softened.
3. Stir in the paprika and rice.
4. Pour over the stock and stir well. Cover and leave on a medium heat for 10 minutes.
5. Add the red pepper, green beans, peas, king prawns and gently mix. Cover and cook for a further 8 minutes.
6. Remove the lid and stir in the Lidl mussels (including the sauce) and place the whole tiger prawns at regular intervals on the top of the paella.
7. Cover and cook for 5 minutes until the shellfish is cooked and heated through.
8. Check the seasoning and add a little sea salt if needed.
9. Top with lemon wedges and serve immediately.

Smoked Salmon, Potato Rösti and Poached Eggs

1 serving 35 minutes

INGREDIENTS

- 1 large potato grated
- 2 slices smoked salmon you can use bacon medallions if you prefer
- salt and pepper to taste
- low calorie cooking spray

For the poached eggs you will need

- 2 medium eggs
- small pan of water
- slotted spoon
- cling film
- ramekin or small bowl/cup
- low calorie cooking spray

DIRECTIONS

FOR THE RÖSTI

1. Grate the potato into a clean tea towel. Fold the towel around the potato to form a ball and squeeze to remove as much moisture as possible, then season.
2. Heat a non stick frying pan over a medium heat and a few sprays of low calorie cooking spray. Place a metal chef's ring or metal pastry cutter inside the frying pan carefully fill with grated potato. Using the back of a spoon, gently push down to make a compact cake. Remove the ring and repeat with the remaining potato. If you use a 2 inch ring you should get 3-4 röstis
3. Fry the rösti for 3-4 minutes on both sides, or until golden-brown all over and tender all the way through.
4. Season with salt, then remove from the pan, place on the plate and top with the smoked salmon.

FOR THE EGGS

1. Fill a small saucepan half-full with water and bring to the boil. Once boiling, lower to medium heat.
2. Tear 2 pieces of cling film (it should be at least double the width of the ramekin) and place the sheet of cling film in a ramekin. Spray with oil, and sprinkle with a little salt and pepper and break the egg into the cling film.
3. Gather up the edges and twist it, making sure that you have the egg enclosed well (you can use a rubber band to secure it). Repeat with the second egg. Carefully place them in the simmering water.
4. Cook for 4 minutes (longer if you don't like your eggs quite so runny) until the egg whites have set. Lift the egg out of the water using a slotted spoon, carefully unwrap the eggs and lift them out of the cling film using a spoon and place them on top of the smoked salmon.

Spicy Salmon Skewers with Cous Cous

 2 servings  20 minutes

INGREDIENTS

- 3 large salmon fillets cut into 16-20 large chunks and skin removed
- 1 125g packet Ainsley Harriott Moroccan Medley Couscous
- 200 ml boiling water
- 1 tsp cumin
- 1/2 tsp paprika
- 6 cherry tomatoes cut in half
- 7 - 8 cm piece cucumber cut into medium dice
- 4 - 5 radish sliced
- 4 spring onions chopped
- 1 small pepper deseeded and choppped
- 1 handful fresh mint chopped
- 1 handful fresh parsley chopped
- 1 handful fresh basil chopped
- 4 tbsp low fat yoghurt
- 1 lemon cut into wedges

DIRECTIONS

1. Put the salmon chunks in a bowl and coat with the cumin and paprika.
2. Thread the salmon onto 4 skewers, we use wooden ones that have been soaked in water to stop them burning in the oven, but you can use metal ones if you want. Squeeze the juice from a couple of lemon wedges over the salmon.
3. Place the completed skewers on a baking tray and cook for 10 minutes at 190-200°C, turning once during cooking.
4. While the skewers are cooking, make up the couscous in a large bowl. One 125g pack will take 200ml of boiling water. Stir, cover with cling film and leave for 3 minutes.
5. When the couscous is ready, stir in the tomatoes, cucumber, radishes, spring onion, peppers and half of the chopped parsley.
6. Set this aside, then in a blender add the yoghurt, remaining herbs and a squeeze of fresh lemon juice.
7. Blitz for a minute or two until the herbs are really fine and the sauce is a nice green colour.
8. Divide the couscous between 2 plates, then serve two salmon skewers on each bed of couscous.
9. Finally drizzle the salmon with a little of the herby yoghurt sauce, garnish with a lemon wedge and enjoy!

Salmon, Broccoli and Potato Bake

 4 servings  45 minutes

INGREDIENTS

- 500 g potatoes cut into wedges
- 1 head broccoli cut into florets and the stalks finely sliced
- 10 tbsp low fat creme fraiche we use Morrisons NuMe Less Than 3% Fat
- ½ red onion very thinly sliced
- 1 bunch asparagus tips
- 4 salmon fillets cut into large chunks
- 8 g dried Parmesan
- sea salt
- freshly ground black pepper

DIRECTIONS

1. Preheat the oven to 200°C
2. Cook the potatoes wedges in some boiling salted water. You can add a fish stock cube to the water for some extra flavour. You could also microwave them for 10 minutes if you prefer. The wedges should be soft when stabbed with a knife
3. Cook the broccoli in some boiling salted water. Again, you can add a fish stock cube to the water for some extra flavour - and you can microwave this for 3 minutes if you prefer. The broccoli should still be quite firm.
4. You can cook the potatoes and broccoli in advance
5. In a large bowl mix together the potato wedges, broccoli, finely sliced onion, asparagus tips and creme fraiche. You can add some more creme fraiche if you need to, but don't forget to add the calories/points.
6. Season with sea salt and freshly ground black pepper, then tip it into a large oven proof dish.
7. Place the salmon chunks on top of the mix, season, sprinkle with the dried parmesan and put it in the oven for 20 minutes or so.
8. When the salmon is just cooked check the dish is piping hot right through and vegetables are cooked through, then remove from the oven and serve with a fresh, crisp salad garnish

Smoked Haddock and Spring Onion Fishcakes

 4 servings  16 minutes

INGREDIENTS

- 500 g potatoes
- 400 g smoked haddock fresh or frozen
- 4-5 spring onions chopped quite finely
- sea salt
- freshly ground black pepper
- low calorie cooking spray
- 30 g panko breadcrumbs
- 1 egg beaten

For the dip

- 8 tbsp fat free Greek yoghurt
- 1 tbsp chives chopped
- 1 tsp mustard powder

DIRECTIONS

1. Wash the potatoes, dry them and prick them several times with a fork Place on a baking tray and bake at 200°C for about an hour, or until the potatoes are soft and fluffy. (You can boil the potatoes if you want, but I find that they can become a bit too moist sometimes so I prefer to bake them)
2. While the potatoes are cooking cook the smoked haddock. You can either poach them, or just pop them in a bowl covered with cling film and microwave them for a few minutes
3. In a small frying pan heat up a few sprays of low calorie cooking spray, then gently sauté the spring onions until they start to soften
4. Drain any moisture from the fish and remove any skin. Flake the fish and check for any bones
5. Mix the haddock and spring onion together and set aside
6. When the potatoes are cooked remove from the oven and allow to cool slightly. Cut each potato in half and scoop out the inside (Or drain them if you're boiling them)
7. Add a couple of sprays of Low calorie cooking spray, then mash the potato until it is quite smooth
8. Add the haddock and spring onion mix to the mashed potato, and season with some sea salt and freshly ground black pepper (don't forget the smoked haddock may be a bit salty so you probably won't need to add too much salt)
9. Divide the mixture into 12 equal portions (you can make them bigger if you want) Roll each one into a ball, then flatten it to form a fishcake shape. Put the shaped fishcakes on a plate and put them in the fridge for 20 minutes or so, until the fishcakes firm up a little
10. Dip each fishcake into beaten egg, then lightly coat it in panko breadcrumbs and place on a clean plate. When you have coated all the fishcakes heat up some Low calorie cooking spray in a frying pan and cook each fishcake for a couple of minutes on each side, or until they start to colour
11. Transfer them on to a baking tray and cook in the oven (on 200 °C) for 10-15 minutes

TO MAKE THE DIP

1. Just mix all the ingredients together and check the taste. You can add some more mustard powder if you want to

Teriyaki Chilli Salmon

 2 servings  40 minutes

INGREDIENTS

- 2 fillets salmon
- low calorie cooking spray
- 2 nests medium egg noodles
- 2 peppers red and yellow
- 1 pak choi chopped
- 1 bunch spring onions chopped
- 150 g mange tout
- 150 g sugar snap peas
- 1 lime

For the Teriyaki Sauce

- 2 tbsp dark soy sauce
- 1 tbsp fish sauce
- 1 tbsp rice vinegar
- 1 tbsp granulated sweetener
- 3 tbsp tomato puree
- 2 cloves garlic minced
- 1 tbsp fresh ginger grated
- 1 lime juice of
- 1/2-1 tsp dried chilli flakes
- 300 ml vegetable stock 300ml/1 ¼ cups boiling water and 1 veg stock cube

DIRECTIONS

1. In a wok or large frying pan heat the garlic and ginger in a little low calorie cooking spray. When they become aromatic add in the soy sauce, fish sauce, rice vinegar, granulated sweetener, tomato puree, lime juice dried chilli flakes, and the vegetable stock. Heat over a high heat for 10 minutes - stirring often
2. Whilst you wait for the sauce to reduce - boil a kettle of water, and pour into a large bowl. Submerge the noodles and set aside. Preheat your oven to 190-200°C ready for the salmon
3. Tip the reduced sauce into a jug (we're going to use half for the salmon and half for the noodles). Wipe down the frying pan, and heat again with a few sprays of Low calorie cooking spray. When VERY hot add the salmon skin side down. Leave the salmon alone for 5 minutes -don't shake the pan, or touch them - just leave them to sizzle
4. Once you start to see the corners of the salmon curl up - it's time to tip in half of the sauce that you put aside. It will spit and bubble, so be careful! Baste the salmon with some of the sauce and place in the pre-heated oven for 10 minutes
5. Now it's time to make the noodles! Drain the noodles off and set aside, we'll be using them in a mo
6. Heat up a wok or frying pan with some Low calorie cooking spray, and tip in the peppers and spring onion. When the spring onion softens, add the mange tout and sugar snap peas. Cook for a few more minutes
7. Add the drained noodles & the rest of the sauce - keep stirring. Add the pak choi and turn the heat down
8. Chop up the lime - slice 3 times (to make 2 slices) and then cut the ends in half to make wedges.
9. Time to check the salmon, lift a flake or 2 in the middle and see if it's cooked. It probably won't be quite ready, so add a lime slice to the top of each fillet, baste with the sauce and put back in the oven for a further 5 minutes. You'll notice the sauce will have gone nice and sticky... this is what we want!
10. Check the salmon again - it should be ready to serve. First plate up the noodles, then top with the salmon, some of the sauce and garnish with the lime wedges!

Salad

Mexican chopped salad 121

Chopped chicken salad 122

Hawaiin pasta salad 123

Tuna mayo salad 124

Seafood salad 125

Jacket potato & mixed beans 126

Rustic potato salad 127

Tuna nicoise salad 128

Tuna & sweetcorn jacket potato 129

Chicken & quinoa salad 130

Roasted teriyaki veg bowl 131

Mexican Chopped Salad

 6 servings  15 minutes

INGREDIENTS

- 1 Romaine Lettuce, chopped
- ½ English Cucumber, chopped
- 1 yellow bell pepper, chopped (or can use red)
- 150g of grape or cherry tomatoes, chopped
- 2 corn on the cobs (in husk)
- 1 small red onion, diced
- 1 handful of fresh cilantro (coriander), finely chopped
- 85g of avocado flesh, diced

For the dressing

- 2 tablespoons of sherry vinegar
- 1 tablespoon of extra virgin olive oil
- 1 tablespoon of maple syrup (can use honey)
- 1 tablespoon of water
- ½ teaspoon of dried oregano
- salt and black pepper to season

DIRECTIONS

1. Place the corn on the cobs (in husks), in the microwave and cook for 5 minutes, remove and allow to cool.
2. Slice off the stem end and then remove husk, use a sharp knife to slice the corn off the cob.
3. Add this to a large bowl with the lettuce, cucumber, pepper, tomatoes, onion, avocado and cilantro
4. Add the oil, vinegar, maple syrup, oregano and water to a small bowl, whisk to all combine, taste and season with a pinch of salt and black pepper.
5. Add this to the salad and toss to coat.

Chopped Chicken Salad

 2 servings  15 minutes

INGREDIENTS

- 3 boneless skinless chicken thighs, raw (approx 250g/8.8oz)
- 1 teaspoon of paprika
- ¼ teaspoon of onion powder
- ¼ teaspoon of garlic powder
- salt and black pepper
- pinch of cayenne (optional)
- olive oil spray
- 1 crisp apple (core removed), sliced thinly
- 1 large carrot, julienned
- 1 head of romaine, chopped
- half a red pepper, chopped into thin strips
- 2 baby cucumbers sliced

for the poppyseed dressing:

- ¼ cup (4 tablespoons) of fat-free plain yoghurt (not Greek)
- juice of half a small lemon
- ½ tablespoon of maple syrup
- ½ teaspoon of yellow mustard
- ½ teaspoon of onion powder
- pinch of poppy seeds
- pinch of salt

DIRECTIONS

1. Add the chicken thighs to a bowl, with the paprika, garlic powder, onion powder and salt and pepper (optional cayenne if you want your chicken spicy)
2. Spray a frying pan over a medium heat with olive oil spray, add the chicken thighs and fry on each side until golden and chicken is cooked through. Remove from pan and set aside to cool slightly, then slice into thin strips.
3. Divide the apple, carrot, lettuce, red pepper, cucumber and chicken equally among too bowls.
4. In a bowl whisk together the poppyseed dressing ingredients.
5. Drizzle it over the salad.

Hawaiian Pasta Salad

 6 servings  25 minutes

INGREDIENTS

- 200g/70z of uncooked pasta (I used farfalle bows)
- 200g/7oz of ham, diced
- 150g/5.5oz of fresh pinepple, chopped
- 4 green onions, chopped
- 1 carrot, julienned
- 2 baby cucumbers, diced
- ½ red pepper, diced
- ½ small red onion diced
- ¾ cup of sweetcorn
- for the dressing:
- 4 tbs of light mayonnaise
- 1.5 cups of fat free plain yoghurt
- 1 tbs of white vinegar
- 2 tsp of dijon mustard
- 2 tbs of sweetener (I used sukrin: 1)
- 1.5 tsps of onion powder
- salt and black pepper to season

DIRECTIONS

1. Add the pasta to a saucepan of boiling hot water, cook to al dente, then drain and set aside to cool.
2. Combine all the ingredients for the dressing and whisk together well.
3. Add all the chopped veg and ham to a large bowl with the pasta.
4. Pour in the dressing and toss to coat.
5. Season well with salt and black pepper

Tuna Mayo Salad

 1 serving  10 minutes

INGREDIENTS

- 140g/5oz of canned Tuna, drained
- 1 tbs of reduced fat mayonnaise
- 3 tbs of quark
- 2 spring onions, sliced
- 1 pickle (gherkin), diced
- pinch of dried dill
- ¼ tsp of onion powder
- juice of half a lemon
- salt and black pepper
- ¼ cup of canned chickpeas
- Chopped romaine lettuce

DIRECTIONS

1. Add all the ingredients apart from the romaine lettuce to a bowl and mix to combine.
2. Serve on a bed of chopped romaine lettuce.

Lemon Garlic Seafood Salad

 2 servings  15 minutes

INGREDIENTS

- 2 cooked boiled eggs, quartered
- 200g of crab sticks (surimi), chopped up
- 5 tablespoons of light mayonnaise
- 1 tablespoon of fresh lemon juice
- ½ teaspoon of garlic granules (powder)
- ½ teaspoon of dried parsley
- salt and black pepper
- 1 romaine lettuce, shredded
- 10 baby plum tomatoes (or grape tomatoes), halved
- 2 baby cucumber, sliced
- 2 green onions (spring onion/scallions), chopped
- ½ green bell pepper, sliced thinly

DIRECTIONS

1. In a bowl mix together the light mayonnaise, granules granules, dried parsley, lemon juice. Add in the chopped crab sticks and mix to combine.
2. Season to taste with salt and black pepper
3. Serve with the boiled eggs, lettuce, tomatoes, cucumber, green bell pepper and green onions
4. Add in the cooked prawns and crab and fold until combined.
5. to two small glass bowls or glasses at some chopped lettuce, along with tomato and cucumber, top with the seafood cocktail and garnish with avocado slices, a slice of lemon and a pinch of cayenne to the top.

Jacket potato with mixed beans and salad

 1 serving 

INGREDIENTS

- 1 large baking potato, scrubbed
- 415g can Heinz Five Beanz in Tomato Sauce (or other Free mixed beans in tomato sauce)
- Mixed salad, to serve

DIRECTIONS

1. Prick the potato all over with a fork. Put in the microwave and cook on high for 10-15 minutes, or until cooked through, turning once halfway.
2. Meanwhile, heat the beans in a saucepan until piping hot.
3. Put the potato on a plate, slice open and top with a generous helping of the beans. Enjoy with lots of salad.

Rustic potato salad

 6 servings  35 minutes

INGREDIENTS

- 750g waxy new potatoes, such as Charlotte
- 4 eggs*
- ½ bunch spring onions, finely chopped
- 4 plum tomatoes, halved, deseeded and roughly chopped
- For the dressing:
- 150g fat-free natural fromage frais
- 1 garlic clove, crushed
- 1 tsp mustard powder mixed with 2 tsp water
- Juice of 1 lemon
- Small handful fresh chives, chopped

DIRECTIONS

1. Cook the potatoes in a saucepan of boiling water for 12-15 minutes or until just tender. Drain well and leave to cool. Halve lengthways and put in a large bowl.
2. At the same time, put the eggs in a small pan and cover with water. Bring to the boil, reduce to a simmer and cook the eggs how you like them (7-8 minutes for just hard-boiled). Cool under cold running water then peel and set aside.
3. Add the spring onions and tomatoes to the potatoes. Roughly chop the eggs and add to the salad, then toss the ingredients together and tip everything into an airtight container.
4. Whisk all the dressing ingredients together and pour into a screw-top jar.
5. Chill the salad and dressing until you're ready to eat, then drizzle the dressing over the salad to serve.

Tuna Nicoise salad

INGREDIENTS

- 200g green beans, trimmed
- 2 little gem lettuces, leaves separated
- 100g each of red and yellow cherry tomatoes, halved
- 1 red onion, thinly sliced
- 2 x small cans tuna in spring water, drained
- 4 eggs, boiled and halved
- For the dressing:
- 4 tbsp fat-free vinaigrette
- 1 level tsp honey
- Juice of 1 lemon
- 1 level tbsp wholegrain mustard

DIRECTIONS

1. Blanch the green beans in a saucepan of lightly salted boiling water for 2-3 minutes, then drain and refresh under cold running water. Drain and transfer to a large bowl with the lettuce, cherry tomatoes and red onion.
2. Break the tuna into bite-size pieces and add to the salad ingredients along with the boiled egg halves.
3. Whisk all the dressing ingredients together and season lightly. Pour the dressing over the salad and toss gently to mix.
4. Cool, cover and chill until you're ready to eat.

Tuna and sweetcorn jacket potato

 4 servings  2 hours 5 minutes

INGREDIENTS

- 4 large jacket potatoes
- 2 x 200g cans of tuna in spring water or brine, drained
- 2 x 198g cans sweetcorn kernels, drained
- 4 level tbsp fat-free natural yogurt
- 4 level tbsp extra-light mayonnaise
- Mixed salad, to serve

DIRECTIONS

1. Preheat the oven to 200°C/fan 180°C/gas 6.
2. Prick the jacket potatoes all over, put them directly on the middle shelf of your oven and cook for 1½-2 hours, or until the skin is really crisp. Alternatively, you can put them in the microwave for 8-10 minutes.
3. When the potatoes are nearly ready, mix the tuna and sweetcorn together with the fat-free natural yogurt and the mayonnaise. Cover and chill until required.
4. Take the jackets out of the oven and cut in half. Fill with the tuna-and-sweetcorn mixture and serve with the mixed salad.

Chicken and quinoa salad

 4 servings  20 minutes

INGREDIENTS

- 200g dried quinoa
- 4 cooked skinless and boneless chicken breasts, roughly shredded
- 4 red apples, cored and cut into bite-sized pieces
- 4 celery sticks, thinly sliced
- Small bag of baby spinach leaves
- Bunch of spring onions, trimmed and thinly sliced
- 2 hard-boiled eggs, peeled and finely chopped, to serve
- Small handful of fresh chives, finely chopped
- Small handful of fresh mint, finely chopped
- For the dressing:
- 200g fat-free natural fromage frais
- 3 tbsp fat-free vinaigrette
- 2 tbsp roughly chopped bottled gherkins

DIRECTIONS

1. Cook the quinoa according to the packet instructions, then drain and set aside.
2. Meanwhile, put the chicken in a large salad bowl with the apples, celery, spinach and spring onions.
3. Mix all of the dressing ingredients together in a bowl and pour over the salad.
4. Add the cooked quinoa and toss to mix well. Scatter over the eggs and fresh herbs to serve.

Roasted teriyaki veg bowl

 4 servings  50 minutes

INGREDIENTS

- 300g long-stemmed broccoli
- 2 baby pak choi, quartered
- 2 red onions, cut into 3cm wedges
- 1 red pepper, deseeded and sliced
- 4 carrots, chopped into wedges
- 400g can chickpeas, drained
- 2 tbsp sesame or olive oil
- 4 tbsp teriyaki sauce
- 1 large thumb-size piece of ginger, grated
- 400g cooked brown rice
- 4 spring onions, finely sliced
- 1 tbsp toasted black and white sesame seeds

DIRECTIONS

1. Heat the oven to 220C/200C fan/gas 7. Chop the broccoli stalks, leaving the florets whole, and put all of it in a large bowl. Add the pak choi, red onions, peppers, carrots, chickpeas (patted dry with kitchen paper), oil, 3 tbsp of the teriyaki sauce and the ginger. Toss until everything is coated and season lightly. Tip onto a large non-stick baking sheet in a single even layer, using two trays if needed.
2. Bake the veg for 35-40 mins, tossing halfway through until starting to brown. When there is 5 mins of cooking time left, heat up the rice. Divide the rice between the bowls and top with the roasted veg. Drizzle over the reserved teriyaki sauce and scatter with the spring onions and sesame seeds.

Desserts

Fruity flapjack cookies 134

Egg custard 135

Oat pancakes 136

Apple betty 137

Pancakes 138

Weetabix cake 139

Chocolate & raspberry custard 140

Brownies 141

Trifle 142

Carrot mug cake 143

Cinnamon bun mug cake 144

Chocolate mug puds 145

Strawberry mouse cheesecake 146

Chocolate cake 147

Custard 148

Eggnog créme brùlées 149

Rice pudding 150

Chocolate waffles 151

Gingerbread biscuits 152

Raspberry & coconut sponge 153

Victoria sponge cake 154

Fruity flapjack cookies

 12 servings  60 minutes

INGREDIENTS

- 125g jumbo oats
- 150g softened butter
- 100g light muscovado sugar
- 1 egg
- 1 tbsp golden syrup
- ½ tsp vanilla extract
- 100g self-raising flour
- 100g mixed dried fruit or raisins
- 75g dried apricots, finely chopped
- 50g desiccated coconut
- ½ tsp ground cinnamon (optional)

DIRECTIONS

1. Heat the oven to 180C/160C fan/gas 4. Scatter the oats over a baking tray and bake for 20 mins, turning once until lightly browned. Remove from the oven and set aside to cool. Tip the butter and sugar into a bowl and beat with an electric whisk for 2 mins until fluffy. Crack in the egg and add the golden syrup and vanilla, then beat until completely combined. Scatter in the flour, all the dried fruit, the coconut, cinnamon (if using), the toasted oats and a pinch of salt. Beat again until everything is combined and you have a thick dough. Use the dough straightaway or cover and chill for up to two days.
2. Line two baking sheets with baking parchment and arrange six large spoonfuls of dough on each, well- spaced apart. Bake for 15 mins (or 18-20 mins if the dough is fridge-cold) until the cookies have spread and are brown at the edges but soft in the middle. Leave to cool on the baking sheet for 5 mins, then transfer to a wire rack and leave to cool completely. Will keep in an airtight container or tin for up to five days.

Egg Custard

4 servings 1 hour 15 minutes
4 hours chilling

INGREDIENTS

- 4 medium eggs
- 600ml skimmed milk
- 1 tsp vanilla extract
- 3 level tbsp sweetener granules
- ½ tsp ground cinnamon, plus a little extra to decorate
- Grated zest and juice of 1 orange
- Pinch of freshly grated nutmeg
- 200g mixed fresh raspberries, blueberries and hulled and halved strawberries, to serve

DIRECTIONS

1. Preheat your oven to 180°C/fan 160°C/gas 4. In a large mixing bowl, whisk the eggs until frothy.
2. In a saucepan, heat the milk, vanilla, sweetener and half the cinnamon until nearly boiling, then pour the mixture into the eggs in a slow drizzle, whisking continuously.
3. Strain the mixture through a sieve into a large measuring jug. Stir in the orange juice and most of the zest, then divide the mixture between 4 ramekins and place on a baking tray. Sprinkle with nutmeg and bake for 50-60 minutes, or until just set.
4. Leave to cool, then chill for 3-4 hours. Sprinkle with the remaining cinnamon and orange zest and serve with the mixed berries

Oat pancakes with berry sauce

12 servings 20 minutes

INGREDIENTS

- 2 large eggs
- 230ml unsweetened almond drink
- 1 level tsp sweetener granules, plus 1 level tsp to serve
- 1 tsp vanilla extract
- 50g porridge oats
- 1 level tsp baking powder
- 50g self-raising flour
- Low-calorie cooking spray

For the sauce:

- 50g blueberries
- 50g raspberries
- 1 level tbsp sweetener granules

DIRECTIONS

1. Preheat your oven to 150°C/fan 130°C/gas 2.
2. Separate the eggs into 2 mixing bowls and, using a fork, whisk the almond drink, sweetener and vanilla extract into the yolks. Stir in the oats and baking powder and leave to soak for 20 minutes.
3. Meanwhile, make the sauce. Blitz the blueberries and raspberries with 1 level tbsp sweetener granules (if you don't have a food processor, mashing them with a fork or potato masher is fine). Press through a fine sieve into a bowl, discarding the seeds in the sieve, and pour the sauce into a jug. Chill until needed.
4. Sift the flour over the oaty mixture and fold it in. Whisk the egg whites into soft peaks and gently fold into the oats using a large metal spoon.
5. Spray a large non-stick frying pan with low-calorie cooking spray and place over a medium heat. When it's hot, add a few large spoonfuls of the batter, spaced well apart (you're aiming to make 12 pancakes altogether). Cook for 2 minutes or until bubbles start to appear in the top of the pancakes and the undersides are nicely golden brown. Flip the pancakes over and cook for another 2 minutes. Put them on a plate, cover with a clean tea towel and keep warm in the oven while you cook the rest.
6. Serve with the sauce (count 1 Syn per level tbsp) and the extra sweetener sprinkled over.

Apple betty

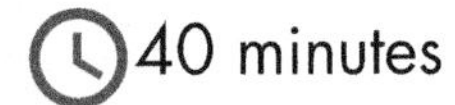

6 servings 40 minutes

INGREDIENTS

- 2 large eating apples, peeled, cored and sliced
- 50g sultanas (or raisins)
- 8 eggs
- 4 level tbsp sweetener granules
- 2 tsp vanilla extract
- 160g no-added-sugar, fat-free vanilla yogurt
- Pinch of cinnamon, to dust
- Fat-free natural fromage frais, to serve

DIRECTIONS

1. Preheat your oven to 190°C/fan 170°C/gas 5. Arrange the apple slices in a 20cm flan dish and sprinkle over most of the sultanas.
2. Beat the eggs with the sweetener and vanilla extract, then add the yogurt and beat again. Pour over the apples and sultanas and allow to sink over the fruit. Scatter over the remaining sultanas, dust with cinnamon and bake for 30 minutes, or until set.
3. Serve warm with the fromage frais.

Pancakes

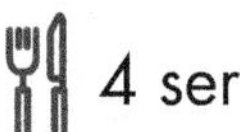 4 servings 40 minutes

INGREDIENTS

- 1 large ripe banana, peeled
- 2 medium eggs, beaten
- 2 level tbsp self-raising flour
- Low-calorie cooking spray
- 200g fresh or frozen mixed berries (defrosted if frozen), to serve
- 100g fat-free natural fromage frais, to serve
- Ground cinnamon, to decorate

DIRECTIONS

1. Mash the banana in a bowl with a fork until smooth, then stir in the eggs and the flour.
2. Spray a small non-stick, heart-shape frying pan with low-calorie cooking spray and put it over a medium heat.
3. Pour a twelfth of the pancake mixture into the pan and cook for 1 minute, or until the base is golden brown. Flip it over then cook for a further 1-2 minutes, or until golden and cooked through. Keep warm while you make 11 more pancakes. Serve 3 pancakes per person with the berries and fromage frais, and dust over the cinnamon.

Weetabix cake

 12 servings 1 hour 10 minutes

INGREDIENTS

- 2 Weetabix
- 200ml skimmed milk
- 100g sultanas
- 100g self-raising flour
- 1 tsp mixed spice
- 2 level tbsp sweetener granules
- 2 large eggs, beaten

DIRECTIONS

1. Preheat your oven to 180°C/fan 160°C/gas 4 and line a 450g loaf tin with non-stick baking paper.
2. Put the Weetabix in a large bowl and pour in the milk. Leave for 2-3 minutes then mash with a fork.
3. Beat in all the remaining ingredients, spoon the mixture into the prepared loaf tin and bake for 1 hour.
4. Cool the cake on a wire rack, turn out and slice into 12 to serve.

Chocolate and raspberry custard

 4 servings  15 minutes

INGREDIENTS

- 1 level tbsp cocoa powder, reserving a large pinch to decorate
- 2 level tbsp cornflour
- 3 level tbsp sweetener granules
- 5 large egg yolks
- 400ml skimmed milk
- ½ tsp vanilla extract
- 20g plain chocolate (at least 70% cocoa), roughly chopped
- 250g fresh raspberries, reserving some to decorate

DIRECTIONS

1. Put the cocoa, cornflour and sweetener in a large mixing bowl, then stir in the egg yolks using a fork until smooth.
2. Using a hand whisk, slowly whisk in the milk, then pour the mixture into a small non-stick saucepan. Place over a medium heat and stir continuously until thickened (it should be thick enough to coat the back of a spoon).
3. Reduce the heat to low, then add the vanilla extract and chocolate, and stir until the chocolate has melted.
4. Tip the raspberries into 4 x 125ml dessert glasses or ramekins and divide over the chocolate custard. Cover loosely with cling film. Leave to cool, then chill for 2 hours, or until set.
5. Remove the cling film and decorate the custards with the remaining raspberries. Evenly dust with the reserved cocoa and serve.

Tip: frozen raspberries taste just as nice as fresh, and they'll last longer

Brownies

 Makes 16  1 hour

INGREDIENTS

- 2 large sweet potatoes (about 500g), peeled and diced
- 100g plain porridge oats
- 3 level tbsp sweetener granules
- 1 medium egg
- 12 soft, pitted dates, roughly chopped
- 2 level tbsp low-fat spread
- 6 tbsp cocoa powder (or raw cacao powder, available in larger supermarkets)
- 16 raspberries
- ½ level tsp icing sugar, to dust

DIRECTIONS

1. Preheat your oven to 180°C/fan 160°C/gas 4 and line the base and sides of an 18cm square loose-bottomed cake tin with non-stick baking paper.
2. Steam the sweet potatoes for 10 minutes or until tender. Leave to cool slightly.
3. Blitz the oats in a food processor until you have fine crumbs. Add the sweetener, egg, dates, spread, cocoa powder and sweet potatoes, season lightly with salt, then whizz to a thick, smooth paste. Pour into the cake tin, smooth the surface and poke in the raspberries, placing them so that each brownie will get 1 raspberry.
4. Bake for 35 minutes, then leave to cool in the tin.
5. Turn out onto a board, then peel away and discard the baking paper. Cut into 16 equal squares and dust evenly with icing sugar to serve.

Tip: If you don't have a steamer, put your sweet potatoes in a colander, cover, then place over a saucepan of boiling water and steam over a high heat.)

Trifle

Makes 8 — 20 minutes+ 6 hours chilling

INGREDIENTS

- 2 x 11.5g sachets sugar-free strawberry jelly crystals
- 100g strawberries, hulled and sliced
- 400g ready-made reduced-fat custard, from a can/carton
- 400g fat-free natural fromage frais
- Fresh mint sprigs, to decorate
- Edible gold glitter/sprinkles, to decorate (optional)

DIRECTIONS

1. Make the jelly according to the pack instructions and allow to cool.
2. Divide the strawberries between 8 individual trifle glasses and pour over the jelly to just cover. Put the glasses in the fridge and chill for a minimum of 6 hours or overnight, until set.
3. To serve, evenly spoon the custard over the jellies and top with the fromage frais. Decorate with the mint sprigs and sprinkle with edible glitter(1 syn per level tsp), if using.

Carrot mug cake

 1 serving 

INGREDIENTS

- 25g self-raising flour
- ¼ tsp mixed spice
- 1 medium egg, separated
- 25g fat-free natural Greek yogurt
- ½ level tbsp sweetener granules
- 50g carrot, coarsely grated
- zest of ¼ of an orange, plus extra to decorate
- ¼ tsp vanilla extract
- pinch of ground cinnamon, to decorate
- For the topping:
- 40g fat-free natural Greek yogurt
- 1 level tsp sweetener granules

DIRECTIONS

1. Mix the flour, mixed spice and a pinch of salt in a small bowl. Using an electric hand whisk, beat the egg white in a clean glass bowl until it forms stiff peaks, then set aside.
2. Put the yogurt, sweetener, carrot, orange zest, vanilla extract and egg yolk in a mixing bowl and mix until well combined. Stir in the flour mixture, then carefully fold in the egg white using a metal spoon.
3. Scrape the mixture into a microwave-safe mug (one that's around 250ml is ideal – try to avoid anything wide and shallow) and cook on High in a 900W microwave for 2 minutes. Leave to cool in the mug until just warm – it will sink a little as it cools.
4. For the topping, mix the yogurt and sweetener together, then spoon it over the just-warm cake. Top with the extra orange zest and cinnamon to serve.

Cinnamon bun mug cake

 1 serving

INGREDIENTS

For the cake:

- 25g self-raising flour
- ½ tsp ground cinnamon
- 1 medium egg, separated
- 25g fat-free natural Greek yogurt
- ½ level tbsp sweetener granules
- 30g raisins (save a few to decorate)
- ¼ tsp vanilla extract

For the topping:

- 40g fat-free natural Greek yogurt
- 1 level tsp sweetener granules
- pinch of cinnamon and remaining raisins, to decorate

DIRECTIONS

1. Mix the flour, cinnamon and raisins in a small bowl.
2. Using an electric hand whisk, beat the egg white in a clean glass bowl until it forms stiff peaks, then set aside.
3. Put the yogurt, sweetener, vanilla extract and egg yolk in a mixing bowl and mix until well combined. Stir in the flour mixture, then carefully fold in the egg white using a metal spoon.
4. Scrape the mixture into a microwave-safe mug (one that's around 250ml is ideal – try to avoid anything wide and shallow) and cook on High in a 900W microwave for 2 minutes. Leave to cool in the mug until just warm – it will sink a little as it cools.
5. For the topping, mix the yogurt and sweetener together, then spoon it over the just-warm cake. Top with a sprinkling of cinnamon and a few raisins.

Chocolate mug puds

 4 servings  10 minutes

INGREDIENTS

- 3 level tbsp cocoa powder
- 3 level tbsp sweetener granules, plus 2 level tsp for the sauce
- 1 level tsp cornflour
- 65g low-fat spread
- 65g self-raising flour
- 2 eggs
- low-calorie cooking spray

DIRECTIONS

1. To make the sauce, put 1 level tbsp cocoa powder, 2 level tsp sweetener and 85ml water in a non-stick saucepan over a medium heat and stir well. Once it's bubbling, mix the cornflour with 1 tbsp water and add to the pan. Cook for 4-5 minutes or until thickened and glossy, stirring occasionally.
2. Meanwhile, cream the remaining sweetener with the spread and mix in the sieved flour, eggs and remaining cocoa.
3. Spray 4 mugs with low-calorie cooking spray and pour in the batter. Cover each mug with cling film, pierce with a fork and cook them one by one in the microwave for 30 seconds on High. Check they're spongy by gently testing them with your finger – if they don't spring back, they might need another 10 seconds. Leave to rest for 1 minute.
4. Turn the puddings out onto plates and pour over the sauce to serve.

Strawberry mousse cheesecake

4 servings 35 minutes+ 4 hours chilling

INGREDIENTS

- 1 large egg white
- 6 digestive biscuits, finely crushed
- 6 sheets leaf gelatine (total weight 10g)
- 3 x 175g pots fat-free no-added-sugar strawberry yogurt
- a few drops of vanilla extract
- a few drops of pink food colouring
- 1 level tsp sweetener granules
- 100g strawberries, hulled and diced, plus 8 small whole strawberries to decorate
- sprigs of mint and 1 level tsp icing sugar, to decorate

DIRECTIONS

1. Preheat your oven to 180°C/fan 160°C/gas 4, line a baking sheet with baking paper and arrange 4 x 7cm pastry rings on top.
2. Lightly whisk the egg white in a bowl. Put the biscuits in another bowl, pour in the egg white and stir. Spoon into the rings and press down well. Bake for 15 minutes, then leave to cool.
3. While the bases are cooling, put the gelatine in a shallow bowl, just cover with cold water and leave to soak for 10-12 minutes, until softened. Squeeze the water out of the gelatine, return it to the bowl and add 6 tbsp just-boiled water. Leave to stand until the gelatine has dissolved.
4. Put the yogurt, vanilla, food colouring and sweetener in a blender. With the motor running, carefully add the gelatine mixture and blend well. Transfer to a bowl and stir in the diced strawberries.
5. Spoon the yogurt mixture over the biscuit bases, cover with cling film and chill for 6-8 hours, or until set. To serve, loosen the edge of each cheesecake with a hot palette knife and turn out onto a plate. Decorate each one with 2 whole strawberries and a mint sprig and evenly dust over the icing sugar.

Chocolate cake

8 servings 30 minutes

INGREDIENTS

- 5 medium eggs, separated
- 50g caster sugar
- 1 tsp vanilla extract
- 60g self-raising flour
- 30g cocoa powder
- ½ tsp baking powder
- 25g milk chocolate
- 250g custard (recipe on the next page)

DIRECTIONS

1. 1. Preheat your oven to 190°C/fan 170°C/gas 5.
2. Line a 20cm x 20cm tin with baking paper. Sit a large, heatproof bowl over a pan of boiling water (ensuring the bowl doesn't touch the water), then turn off the heat. Put the egg whites and sugar in the bowl and beat until they form stiff peaks.
3. Add the egg yolks and vanilla extract to the bowl and whisk them for 2-3 minutes, until thick and glossy. Remove the bowl from the pan, sift in the flour, cocoa powder and baking powder and fold them in using a metal spoon.
4. Pour the mixture into the tin, shaking the tin a little to level it out. Bake for 10-12 minutes, or until the sponge is risen and set, then allow to cool slightly.
5. At the same time, melt the chocolate in a heatproof bowl over a pan of gently simmering water (ensuring the bowl doesn't touch the water), stirring it occasionally. Evenly drizzle the melted chocolate over the sponge and leave it to cool slightly. While it's cooling, follow our recipe to make the Slimming World custard. Cut the sponge into 8 equal portions and serve with the hot custard.

Custard

INGREDIENTS

- 400ml semi-skimmed milk
- 6 large egg yolks
- 2 level tbsp sweetener granules
- 1 level tbsp cornflour
- 1 tsp vanilla extract

DIRECTIONS

1. Bring the milk to the boil in a small non-stick saucepan over a medium heat. Whisk the egg yolks and sweetener together in a heatproof bowl until thick and pale, then gradually whisk in the cornflour.
2. Slowly stir in the boiling milk and vanilla extract. Return the mixture to a clean pan and stir over a low heat until the mixture thickens and coats the back of a rubber spatula or wooden spoon. Pour the custard through a sieve into a clean bowl or jug – and enjoy!

Eggnog crème brûlées

4 servings 10 minutes

INGREDIENTS

- 100g low-fat custard from a can or carton
- 3 level tbsp advocaat
- 125g plain quark
- ¼ tsp freshly grated nutmeg
- 1 level tsp sweetener granules
- 2 level tbsp granulated sugar

DIRECTIONS

1. Grab a bowl and mix your custard, advocaat, quark, nutmeg and sweetener together until smooth.
2. Divide your mixture equally between 4 x 7cm heatproof ramekins, ensuring that the tops are level. Cover your brûlées and put in the fridge until needed.
3. Shortly before serving, add the sugar and 1 tbsp cold water to a small stainless-steel pan. Keep stirring over a low heat until the sugar has dissolved and the syrup is clear. Increase the heat and boil rapidly until the syrup has turned a caramel colour.
4. Remove the pan from the heat and briefly plunge the base into cold water. (If the caramel sets on the base of the pan, just return to a low heat until it's liquid again.) Quickly drizzle the caramel evenly over the top of each brûlée – once set, it's time to get cracking with your spoon!

Rice pudding

 4 servings

2 hours 10 minutes

INGREDIENTS

- low-calorie cooking spray
- 100g plain dried pudding rice
- 2 level tbsp sweetener granules
- 650ml skimmed milk
- 1 tsp freshly grated nutmeg, plus extra to decorate
- 1 tsp ground cinnamon
- 1 mango, peeled, stone removed and sliced

DIRECTIONS

1. Preheat your oven to 150°C/fan 130°C/gas 2 and lightly spray a medium baking dish with low-calorie cooking spray.
2. Put the rice in a large sieve and rinse under cold water for 1-2 minutes. Drain and transfer to the baking dish. Add the sweetener and pour over the milk. Stir well, then sprinkle over the spices.
3. Bake the pudding for 1 hour, then stir and return to the oven for 30 minutes. Stir again, then bake for a further 30 minutes, or until lightly browned. Serve warm in cups or bowls, with a little grated nutmeg and the mango.

Chocolate waffles

Makes 6 20 minutes

INGREDIENTS

- 2 medium eggs, separated
- 2 level tbsp cocoa powder
- 50g self-raising flour
- 2 x 115g pots fat-free no-added-sugar flavoured yogurt (chocolate, white chocolate, raspberry or vanilla will all work well)
- 2 level tsp icing sugar, to dust (optional – add 1 Syn per serving)

DIRECTIONS

1. Preheat your oven to 220°C/fan 200°C/gas 7.
2. Mix the egg yolks, cocoa powder, flour and 4 tbsp yogurt in a bowl until smooth. Whisk the egg whites in a clean bowl until stiff peaks form, then fold through the flour mixture until combined.
3. Divide the mixture between 6 individual silicone waffle moulds.
4. Cook the waffles on a non-stick baking tray in an oven preheated to 220°C/fan 200°C/gas 7 for 7-8 minutes until firm to the touch.
5. Carefully turn the waffles out onto a plate and serve with the remaining yogurt and fresh raspberries. Dust with 2 level tsp of icing sugar, if you like.

Gingerbread biscuits

Makes 60 45 minutes

INGREDIENTS

- 50g unsalted butter
- 2 level tbsp golden syrup
- 2 level tbsp light soft brown sugar
- 225g self-raising flour
- 1 tbsp ground ginger
- 1 tsp ground cinnamon
- ¼ tsp ground cloves
- 2 level tsp sweetener granules
- 3 level tbsp skimmed milk
- 1 level tsp icing sugar, for dusting

DIRECTIONS

1. Preheat your oven to 190°C/fan 170°C/gas 5 and cover 2 large baking trays with non-stick baking paper. Melt the butter and golden syrup in a small non-stick pan over a low heat, then remove from the heat, stir in the sugar and set aside.
2. Sift the flour, spices and ¼ tsp salt into a bowl, then stir in the sweetener. Add the melted butter and milk and stir into a dough. Knead until smooth, then halve the dough with a knife.
3. Roll out 1 piece of dough between 2 large sheets of cling film to a thickness of about 3-4mm. Use a 5cm x 5cm (or 6cm x 4cm) cutter to cut out as many biscuits as you can. Lightly re-knead and roll out the trimmings again and again, until all the dough is used up. Repeat with the second piece of dough until you have about 60 biscuits.
4. Arrange the biscuits on the baking trays and bake on the middle shelf of the oven for about 7½ minutes or until they're starting to brown but are still slightly soft to the touch. Leave to cool, then dust with icing sugar and store in an airtight container.

Raspberry and coconut sponge

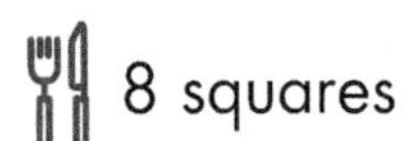

8 squares 30 minutes

INGREDIENTS

- 4 large eggs
- 50g granulated sugar
- 1 tsp vanilla extract
- 100g self-raising flour
- 4 level tbsp reduced-sugar raspberry jam
- 25g desiccated coconut
- 8 fresh raspberries, to decorate, plus extra to serve

DIRECTIONS

1. Preheat your oven to 190°C/fan 170°C/gas 5 and line a 20cm x 30cm cake tin with baking paper. In a mixing bowl, use an electric hand whisk to beat the eggs and sugar for 5-8 minutes, until the mixture doubles in volume, is thick, light and foamy, and leaves a trail when you lift the whisk.
2. Add the vanilla extract, sift in the flour, then gently fold everything together. Pour the mixture into the tin and bake for 10-15 minutes, until risen and shrinking away from the sides. Leave to cool completely in the tin.
3. Once cool, take the sponge out of the tin and carefully remove the paper. Spread the jam evenly over the sponge, then sprinkle the coconut over the top. Cut into 8 equal pieces and add a raspberry to each one. Serve with the extra raspberries.

Victoria sponge cake

10 servings 50 minutes

INGREDIENTS

- 200g low-fat spread suitable for baking
- 6 level tbsp sweetener
- 4 eggs
- few drops of vanilla essence
- 200g self-raising flour
- 200g plain quark
- 175g no-added-sugar, fat-free strawberry yogurt
- 500g strawberries
- 1 level tsp icing sugar, to dust

DIRECTIONS

1. Preheat your oven to 180°C/fan 160°C/gas 4. Line 2 x 20cm cake tins with greaseproof paper. Mix the spread with the sweetener until smooth and then gradually beat in the eggs and vanilla essence. Sift the flour and fold into the mixture.
2. 2. Divide the mixture between the cake tins and bake for 25-30 minutes (until the sponge springs back when lightly touched). Remove from the oven and turn out onto a wire rack to cool completely.
3. 3. Mix the quark with the yogurt; halve most of the strawberries and slice the remainder. Place one sponge on a plate, top with the strawberry halves and pour over the yogurt mixture. Place the second sponge on top and decorate with the sliced strawberries. Dust with a little icing sugar and slice into 10 equal portions to serve.

Printed in Great Britain
by Amazon